INTERNATIONAL CUISINE

INTERNATIONAL CUISINE
soups & salads

JG PRESS

Published by World Publications Group, Inc.
455 Somerset Avenue
North Dighton, MA 02764
www.wrldpub.net

All interior photographs courtesy of Sunset Books.
Cover photograph: ©Michael Deuson/ Foodpix

ISBN 1-57215-453-5

Editors: Joel Carino and Emily Zelner
Designers: Lynne Yeamans and Stephanie Stislow
Production Director: Ellen Milionis

Printed and bound in China by SNP Leefung Printers Limited.

1 2 3 4 5 06 05 03 02

contents

soups

minestrone genovese

preparation time: about 1 hour

Pesto (recipe follows)

2 large leeks

12 cups fat-free reduced-sodium chicken broth

2 large carrots, thinly sliced

2 large stalks celery, thinly sliced

2 cans (about 15 oz. *each*) cannellini (white kidney beans), drained

10 ounces (about 2 ½ cups) dried medium-size elbow macaroni

³/₄ pound yellow crookneck squash or zucchini, cut into ¹/₂-inch chunks

1 large red bell pepper, seeded and cut into ¹/₂-inch pieces

2 packages (about 10 oz. *each*) frozen tiny peas

Basil sprigs

Salt and pepper

1 Prepare Pesto.

2 Cut off and discard root ends and green tops of leeks. Discard coarse outer leaves. Split leeks in half lengthwise and rinse well; thinly slice crosswise.

3 Combine leeks, broth, carrots, and celery in an 8- to 10-quart pan. Bring to a boil over high heat; reduce heat, cover, and simmer for 10 minutes.

4 Stir in beans, pasta, squash, and bell pepper; cover and simmer just until pasta is tender to bite (about 10 more minutes).

5 Add peas and bring to a boil. Stir in ½ cup of the Pesto into soup. Serve hot or at room temperature if made ahead, let cool and then cover and refrigerate for up to a day; bring to room temperature or reheat before serving. Garnish with basil. Offer salt, pepper, and remaining Pesto to add to taste.

makes 12 servings

PESTO

In a food processor or blender, combine 2 cups lightly packed fresh basil, 1 cup freshly grated Parmesan cheese, ¼ cup olive oil, 2 tablespoons pine nuts or slivered almonds, and 1 or 2 cloves garlic. Whirl until smooth. Season to taste with salt. If made ahead, cover and refrigerate for up to a day.

makes 1 cup

per serving: 322 calories, 17 g protein, 46 g carbohydrates, 9 g total fat, 5 mg cholesterol, 957 mg sodium

---

homemade chicken broth

preparation time: about 20 minutes
cooking time: about 3 hours
chilling time: at least 4 hours

---

5 pounds bony chicken pieces

2 large onions, cut into chunks

2 large carrots, cut into chunks

6 to 8 parsley sprigs

¹/₂ teaspoon whole black peppercorns

1 Rinse chicken and place in a 6- to 8-quart pan. Add onions, carrots, parsley sprigs, peppercorns, and 3 ½ quarts water. Bring to a boil over high heat; then reduce heat, cover, and simmer for 3 hours. Let cool.

2 Pour broth through a fine strainer into a bowl; discard residue. Cover broth; refrigerate for at least 4 hours or up to 2 days. Lift off and discard fat. To store, freeze in 1- to 4-cup portions.

makes about 10 cups

per cup: Due to variations in ingredients and cooking time, precise nutritional data is not available. The nutritional value of this broth is similar to that of canned low-sodium chicken broth.

chard soup with beans & orzo

preparation time: about 1 1/2 hours

1 pound pear-shaped (Roma-type) tomatoes

2 tablespoons olive oil

1 large onion, chopped

1 clove garlic, minced or pressed

2 medium-size stalks celery, diced

2 ounces thinly sliced prosciutto or cooked ham, slivered

12 cups beef broth

2 large carrots, diced

1 tablespoon minced fresh rosemary or
   1 teaspoon dried rosemary

1 pound Swiss chard, coarse stems removed

3 cans (about 15 oz. *each*) pinto beans, drained and rinsed

8 ounces green beans, cut info 1-inch lengths

1 pound zucchini, cut into 3/4-inch chunks

4 ounces (about 2/3 cup) dried orzo or other rice-shaped pasta

Freshly grated Parmesan cheese

Salt and pepper

1 Bring 4 cups water to a boil in an 8- to 10-quart pan over high heat. Drop tomatoes into water and cook for 1 minute. Lift out; peel and discard skin. Chop tomatoes and set aside. Discard water.

2 Heat oil in pan over medium-high heat. Add onion, garlic, celery, and prosciutto. Cook, stirring often, until onion is soft (5 to 8 minutes). Add broth, carrots, and rosemary. Bring to a boil; reduce heat, cover, and simmer for 10 minutes. Meanwhile, cut chard crosswise into 1/2-inch strips. Mash 1 can of the pinto beans.

3 Add mashed and whole pinto beans, green beans, zucchini, and tomatoes to pan; stir well. Cover and simmer for 5 more minutes.

4 Stir in chard and pasta; simmer, uncovered, just until pasta is tender to bite (about 10 more minutes). Serve hot or at room temperature. If made ahead, let cool and then cover and refrigerate for up to a day; bring to room temperature or reheat before serving.

5 Offer cheese, salt, and pepper to add to taste.

makes 10 to 12 servings

per serving: 210 calories, 11 g protein, 30 g carbohydrates, 5 g total fat, 4 mg cholesterol, 2,179 mg sodium

STORING HOMEMADE SOUP: Let hot soup cook, uncovered; then cover and keep refrigerated for up to 3 days. For longer storage, ladle the cooled soup into glass jars or freezer containers, making sure to leave at least an inch of head space at the top of the container to allow for expansion. Close containers airtight and label before freezing; use soup within 3 months. To thaw frozen soup, let it stand overnight in the refrigerator; then reheat over medium heat, stirring occasionally. Never try to rush reheating—the soup needs to heat evenly. Slow reheating is especially important for soups made with milk, cream, or cheese, in which the ingredients may separate.

goulash soup

preparation time: about 2 ½ hours

1 pound boneless beef round tip, trimmed of fat

2 medium-size onions, finely chopped

1 clove garlic, minced or pressed

1 teaspoon salad oil

1 tablespoon sweet Hungarian paprika

½ teaspoon dry marjoram leaves

5 cups water

2 tablespoons all-purpose flour

3 beef bouillon cubes

2 small thin-skinned potatoes, cut into ½-inch cubes

1 medium-size red bell pepper, seeded and finely chopped

Salt and white pepper

¼ cup chopped parsley

1 Cut beef into ½-inch cubes. In a 3 ½- to 4-quart pan, combine beef, onions, garlic, oil, paprika, marjoram, and ½ cup of the water. Cover and simmer over medium-low heat for 30 minutes. Uncover and increase heat to medium; cook, stirring often, until liquid has evaporated and onions are browned (20 to 25 minutes).

2 Stir in flour until smoothly blended. Add 1 cup more of the water and bouillon cubes, stirring to dissolve bouillon and loosen any browned bits in pan. Gradually blend in remaining 3 ½ cups water and bring to a boil. Add potatoes and bell pepper. Reduce heat, cover, and simmer, stirring occasionally, until meat is very tender (1 to 1 ½ hours). Skim and discard surface fat, if necessary. Season to taste with salt and pepper. Stir in parsley.

makes 4 servings

per serving: 264 calories, 27 g protein, 24 g carbohydrates, 6 g total fat, 68 mg cholesterol, 664 mg sodium

caribbean corn chowder

preparation time: about 30 minutes

1 tablespoon salad oil

1 large onion, finely chopped

1 large red bell pepper, seeded and chopped

3 large fresh green Anaheim or other large mild chiles, seeded and chopped

5 ½ cups low-sodium chicken broth

2 tablespoons minced fresh tarragon or 1 teaspoon dry tarragon

¼ teaspoon pepper

5 large ears corns, husks and silk removed

Tarragon sprigs (optional)

1 Heat oil in a 5- to 6-quart pan over medium-high heat. Add onion, bell pepper, and chiles. Cook, stirring often, until onion is soft (about 5 minutes). Add broth, minced tarragon, and pepper; bring to a boil. Meanwhile, cut corn kernels from cobs.

2 Add corn to boiling broth mixture. Reduce heat, cover, and simmer until corn is hot (about 5 minutes). If made ahead, let cool; then cover and refrigerate for up to 1 day. Serve hot or cool.

3 To serve, ladle soup into bowls; garnish with tarragon sprigs, if desired.

makes 6 servings

per serving: 165 calories, 6 g protein, 28 g carbohydrates, 5 g total fat, 0 mg cholesterol, 67 mg sodium

winter minestrone

preparation time: about 20 minutes
cooking time: about 1 hour and 5 minutes

2 tablespoons olive oil

1 large onion, finely chopped

1 large celery stalk, finely chopped

2 large cloves garlic, minced or pressed

1 teaspoon dry basil leaves

1/2 teaspoon *each* dry rosemary, dry oregano
    leaves, and dry thyme leaves

1/4 cup pearl barley

2 large thin-skinned potatoes, diced

3 large carrots, diced

8 cups low-sodium chicken broth

1 large turnip, peeled and diced

1 can (about 15 oz.) cannellini (white kidney beans)
    or red kidney beans, drained and rinsed

2/3 cup small shell pasta or elbow macaroni

1/4 cup tomato paste

2 cups finely shredded green cabbage

Grated Parmesan cheese

1 Heat oil in a 5- to 6-quart pan over medium-high heat. Add onion, celery, garlic, basil, rosemary, oregano, and thyme. Cook, stirring, until onion is soft (about 5 minutes). Add barley, potatoes, carrots, and chicken broth; bring to a boil over high heat. Reduce heat, cover, and simmer for 20 minutes. Add turnip. Cover and simmer for 20 more minutes.

2 Stir in beans, pasta, and tomato paste. Bring to a boil over high heat; reduce heat, cover, and simmer until pasta is al dente (about 15 minutes). Add cabbage and simmer, uncovered, until tender-crisp (about 5 more minutes). Ladle into bowls and offer with Parmesan.

makes 8 to 10 servings

per serving: 241 calories, 9 g protein, 41 g carbohydrates, 5 g total fat, 0 mg cholesterol, 314 mg sodium

SOUP GARNISHES ADD PIZZAZZ: Looking for soup garnishes? Just about anything goes: a dollop of sour cream or yogurt, a pat of plain or flavored butter, snipped chives or minced parsley, sliced green onion or ripe olives, chopped fresh herbs, sliced almonds, lemon or orange slices, crumbled cooked bacon, small cooked shrimp, grated cheese, crisp seasoned croutons. You can sprinkle garnishes over soup in a tureen or into individual bowls. Or pass toppings at the table and let diners garnish their own bowlfuls. (This is the best way to serve cheese and croutons—unless you sprinkle them over the soup just before serving, you may end up with stringy cheese or soggy croutons.)

leek soup with brie

preparation time: about 1¼ hours

Toasted French Bread (recipe follows)

6 to 9 large leeks

2 tablespoons butter or margarine

8 ounces mushrooms, thinly sliced

1 clove garlic, minced or pressed

½ teaspoon dry tarragon

¼ teaspoon ground white pepper

2 ½ tablespoons unbleached all-purpose flour

1 quart homemade or canned vegetable broth

⅓ cup whipping cream

6 ounces Brie cheese

1 Prepare Toasted French Bread.

2 Cut off and discard root ends of leeks. Trim tops, leaving about 3 inches of green leaves. Discard coarse outer leaves. Split leeks in half lengthwise and rinse well. Thinly slice (you should have about 2 quarts).

3 Melt butter in a 4- to 5-quart pan over medium heat. Add leeks, mushrooms, garlic, tarragon, and pepper. Cook, stirring occasionally, until vegetables are very soft and most of the liquid has evaporated (about 15 minutes).

4 Add flour and cook, stirring, until bubbly. Remove from heat and gradually stir in broth and cream. Return to heat and bring to a boil, stirring constantly.

5 Ladle soup into 6 heatproof 1 ½- to 2-cup soup bowls. Top each serving with a piece of Toasted French Bread buttered side up.

6 Slice Brie ½ inch thick; place a cheese slice on each toast slice. Bake in a 425° oven until bubbly (about 10 minutes). Then broil about 6 inches below heat until lightly browned (1 to 2 minutes).

makes 6 servings

TOASTED FRENCH BREAD

Cut 6 slices (each about ½ inch thick) from a loaf of French bread. Arrange slices in a single layer on a baking sheet. Bake in a 325° oven until dry (20 to 25 minutes). Spread one side with butter or margarine, using ½ teaspoon for each slice. (At this point, you may wrap in foil and let stand at room temperature for up to a day.)

per serving: 357 calories, 11 g protein, 37 g carbohydrates, 20 g total fat , 59 mg cholesterol, 1,048 mg sodium

cream beet borscht

preparation time: 10 minutes

2 cans (about 15 oz. *each*) pickled beets

About 4 cups plain nonfat yogurt

1 cup vegetable broth

Dill sprigs

Pepper

1 Drain beets, reserving 1 ½ cups of the liquid. In a large bowl, combine beets, reserved liquid, 4 cups of the yogurt, and broth. In a food processor or blender, whirl beet mixture, about a third at a time, until smoothly puréed. If made ahead, cover and refrigerate until next day.

2 Serve borscht cool or cold. To serve, ladle into wide bowls. Add yogurt to taste and garnish with dill sprigs. Season to taste with pepper.

makes 6 to 8 servings

per serving: 113 calories, 8 g protein, 19 g carbohydrates, 0.5 g total fat, 3 mg cholesterol, 582 mg sodium

ruote & meatball soup

preparation time: about 1 hour

Herbed Meatballs (recipe follows)

14 cups fat-free reduced-sodium chicken broth

1/3 cup reduced-sodium soy sauce

1/3 cup lightly packed brown sugar

3 tablespoons smooth peanut butter

1/4 cup distilled white vinegar (or to taste)

10 ounces (about 4 1/2 cups) dried ruote or other medium-size pasta shape

12 ounces spinach (about 3 cups lightly packed), coarse stems removed, rinsed, and drained

1/2 cup chopped red bell pepper

1 teaspoon Asian sesame oil (or to taste)

Cilantro

Crushed red pepper flakes

1 Prepare Herbed Meatballs.

2 Combine broth, soy sauce, sugar, peanut butter, and vinegar in a 6- to 8-quart pan. Bring to a boil over high heat, stirring occasionally with a whisk. Stir in meatballs and pasta; reduce heat and boil gently just until pasta is tender to bite (8 to 10 minutes; or according to package directions).

3 Add spinach and bell pepper. Cook just until heated through (about 3 minutes). Add sesame oil and ladle into bowls. Garnish with cilantro. Offer pepper flakes to add to taste.

makes 8 to 10 servings

HERBED MEATBALLS

In a large bowl, combine 1 pound fresh ground turkey breast, 1/2 cup cooked couscous, 1/4 cup all-purpose flour, 1/4 cup water, and 1/2 teaspoon ground coriander or dried basil. Mix well. Shape into 1- to 1 1/2-inch balls. Place balls slightly apart in a lightly oiled 10- by 15-inch baking pan. Bake in a 450° oven until well browned (about 15 minutes). Pour off any fat. Keep warm.

per serving: 276 calories, 20 g protein, 40 g carbohydrates, 5 g total fat, 29 mg cholesterol, 444 mg sodium

leek & green onion chowder

preparation time: about 50 minutes

3 pounds leeks

1 tablespoon butter or margarine

2 tablespoons all-purpose flour

1/2 teaspoon ground white pepper

6 cups low-sodium chicken broth

3 cups thinly sliced green onions

3 tablespoons lemon juice

Salt

Thin lemon slices

Reduced-fat sour cream

1 Trim ends and all but 3 inches of green tops from leeks; remove tough outer leaves. Split leeks lengthwise; rinse well, then thinly slice crosswise.

2 Melt butter in a 5- to 6-quart pan over medium-high heat. Add leeks; cook, stirring often, until soft (8 to 10 minutes). Stir in flour and white pepper; then stir in broth, bring to a boil over high heat, stirring. Add onions, cook, stirring, just until onions turn bright green (about 2 minutes). Stir in lemon juice and season to taste with salt.

3 To serve, ladle soup into bowls. Garnish each serving with lemon slices and a dollop of sour cream.

makes 6 servings

per serving: 136 calories, 5 g protein, 22 g carbohydrates, 4 g total fat, 5 mg cholesterol, 102 mg sodium

pistou soup with split peas

preparation time: about 35 minutes
cooking time: about 1 1/2 hours

1 pound large leeks

2 tablespoons olive oil

1 cup chopped carrots

1/8 to 1/4 teaspoon ground red pepper (cayenne)

2 medium-size thin-skinned potatoes, peeled and diced

2/3 cup green split peas, rinsed and drained

1 1/2 quarts homemade or canned vegetable broth

1 1/2 quarts water

Pistou (recipe follows)

1 cup frozen cut green beans

2/3 cup 2-inch pieces dry spaghetti

Grated Parmesan cheese (optional)

1 Cut off and discard root ends of leeks. Trim tops, leaving about 3 inches of green leaves. Discard coarse outer leaves. Split leeks in half lengthwise and rinse well. Thinly slice.

2 Heat oil in a 6- to 8-quart pan over medium heat. Stir in leeks, carrots, and ground red pepper. Cook, stirring often, until leeks are soft but not browned (6 to 8 minutes).

3 Stir in potatoes, split peas, broth, and water. Bring to a boil; reduce heat, cover, and simmer until peas are tender to bite (about 1 hour). Meanwhile, prepare Pistou.

4 Stir beans, spaghetti, and Pistou into soup. Increase heat to medium-high and boil gently, uncovered, until spaghetti is just tender to bite (8 to 10 minutes). Serve with cheese to add to taste, if desired.

makes 6 to 8 servings

PISTOU

In a medium-size bowl, combine 4 cloves garlic, minced or pressed; 1 can (about 6 oz.) tomato paste; 3/4 cup grated Parmesan cheese, 1/4 cup minced parsley; 1 1/2 tablespoons dry basil; and 1/4 cup olive oil. Stir well.

per serving: 359 calories, 13 g protein, 44 g carbohydrates, 16 g total fat, 7 mg cholesterol, 1,241 mg sodium

spirited cherry soup

preparation time: about 25 minutes

4 cups pitted light or dark sweet cherries (or use some of each)

3 1/2 cups white grape juice

2 teaspoons grated lemon peel

2 tablespoons lemon juice

3 tablespoons orange-flavored liqueur or 1 1/2 teaspoons grated orange peel

Mint sprigs and thin strips of orange peel (optional)

1 Divide cherries among 4 bowls.

2 In a 2- to 3-quart pan, combine grape juice and lemon peel; bring to a boil over high heat. Stir in lemon juice and liqueur; then pour juice mixture equally over cherries. Garnish each serving with mint sprigs and orange peel, if desired.

makes 4 servings

per serving: 278 calories, 2 g protein, 63 g carbohydrates, 1 g total fat, 0 mg cholesterol, 79 mg sodium

black bean soup

preparation time: about 40 minutes

SOUP:

2 teaspoons vegetable oil

1 large onion, chopped

1 ³/₄ or 2 ³/₄ cups fat-free reduced-sodium chicken broth

1 large can (about 28 oz.) tomatoes

3 cans (about 15 oz. *each*) black beans, drained, rinsed, and puréed; or 1 package (about 7 oz.) instant refried black bean mix

1 fresh jalapeño chile, seeded and minced

2 teaspoons cumin seeds

CONDIMENTS:

Cheddar cheese

Plain nonfat yogurt

Cilantro leaves

Lime wedges

1 In a 5- to 6-quart pan, combine oil and onion. Cook over medium heat, stirring often, until onion is deep golden (about 20 minutes). Add 1 ¾ cups broth (or 2 ¾ cups if using instant beans).

2 Add tomatoes and their liquid to pan; break tomatoes up with a spoon. Stir in beans, chile, and cumin seeds. Bring to a boil; then reduce heat and simmer, uncovered, until soup is thick and flavors are blended (7 to 10 minutes).

3 To serve, ladle soup into bowls. Add condiments to taste.

makes 4 servings

per serving: 327 calories , 21 g protein, 51 g carbohydrates, 6 g total fat, 0 mg cholesterol, 795 mg sodium

chilled cucumber & cilantro soup

preparation time: about 10 minutes
chilling time: at least 2 hours

1 very large cucumber, peeled and cut into chunks

1 ¹/₄ cups low-sodium chicken broth

³/₄ cup firmly packed cilantro leaves

¹/₂ cup nonfat or low-fat milk

¹/₂ cup lemon juice

Salt

1 In a food processor or blender, combine cucumber, broth, cilantro, milk, and lemon juice; whirl until smoothly puréed, Season purée to taste with salt.

2 Cover and refrigerate until cold (at least 2 hours) or until next day.

3 To serve, ladle into bowls.

makes 4 servings

per serving: 36 calories, 3 g protein, 6 g carbohydrates, 1 g total fat, 0.6 mg cholesterol, 62 mg sodium

tomato, beef & orzo soup

preparation time: about 1 3/4 hours

1 teaspoon olive oil or salad oil

1 pound lean boneless beef cut into 3/4-inch chunks

About 5 cups beef broth

1 small onion, chopped

1 1/2 teaspoons dried thyme

1 can (about 6 oz.) tomato paste

4 ounces (about 2/3 cup) dried orzo or other rice-shaped pasta

1 large tomato, chopped

2 tablespoons dry red wine (or to taste)

Cilantro

Salt and pepper

1 Heat oil in a 4- to 5-quart pan over medium heat. Add beef and cook, stirring, until browned (about 10 minutes); if pan appears dry, stir in water, 1 tablespoon at a time. Add 1 cup of the broth; stir to loosen browned bits. Bring to a boil over high heat; reduce heat, cover, and simmer for 30 minutes.

2 Add onion and thyme. Cook, uncovered, over medium-high heat, stirring often, until liquid has evaporated and pan drippings are richly browned (about 10 minutes). Add 4 cups more broth and tomato paste. Bring to a boil over high heat, stirring to loosen browned bits; reduce heat, cover, and boil gently for 20 more minutes.

3 Add pasta, cover, and continue to cook, stirring often, just until pasta is tender to bite (8 to 10 minutes; or according to package directions). Stir in tomato. If soup is too thick, add a little broth or water; if too thin, continue to simmer until thickened. Remove from heat and add wine. Ladle into bowls. Garnish with cilantro. Offer salt and pepper to add to taste.

makes 4 or 5 servings

per serving: 300 calories, 23 g protein, 28 g carbohydrates, 9 g total fat, 59 mg cholesterol, 1,985 mg sodium

mushroom barley soup

preparation time: about 1 1/2 hours

1 tablespoon salad oil or olive oil

1 pound mushrooms, thinly sliced

1 large onion, chopped

2 medium-size carrots, thinly sliced

10 cups vegetable broth

1 cup pearl barley, rinsed and drained

1 tablespoon finely chopped fresh oregano or 1 teaspoon dried oregano

8 ounces red or green Swiss chard

Pepper

1 Heat oil in a 5- to 6-quart pan over medium-high heat. Add mushrooms, onion, and carrots. Cook, stirring often, until vegetables are soft and almost all liquid has evaporated (about 25 minutes). Add broth, barley, and oregano. Bring to a boil over high heat; then reduce heat, cover, and simmer until barley is tender to bite (about 30 minutes).

2 Meanwhile, trim and discard discolored stem ends from chard. Rinse chard and drain well; then coarsely chop leaves and stems.

3 Stir chard into soup and simmer, uncovered, until leaves are limp and bright green (5 to 10 minutes). Ladle soup into bowls; season to taste with pepper:

makes 6 to 8 servings

per serving: 196 calories, 5 g protein, 37 g carbohydrates, 4 g total fat, 0 mg cholesterol, 1,512 mg sodium

tortellini & escarole soup

preparation time: 45 minutes

1 tablespoon olive oil

1 large onion, chopped

2 large carrots, chopped

1 strip lemon zest, about ¼ inch by 4 inches

10 cups fat-free reduced-sodium chicken broth;

1 package (about 9 oz.) fresh cheese or meat tortellini or ravioli

1 package (about 10 oz.) frozen tiny peas, thawed

8 ounces (about 6 cups) shredded escarole

Freshly grated or ground nutmeg

Lemon wedges

Salt

1 Heat oil in a 5- to 6-quart pan over medium-high heat. Add onion, carrots, and lemon zest. Cook, stirring, until onion is soft (5 to 8 minutes).

2 Add broth and bring to a boil over high heat. Add pasta; reduce heat and boil gently, stirring occasionally, just until pasta is tender to bite (4 to 6 minutes; or according to package directions).

3 Stir in peas and escarole; cook just until escarole is wilted (1 to 2 minutes). Remove and discard zest.

4 Ladle soup into bowls. Dust generously with nutmeg. Offer lemon and salt to add to taste.

makes 8 servings

per serving: 193 calories, 11 g protein, 27 g carbohydrates, 7 g total fat, 13 mg cholesterol, 316 mg sodium

spring vegetable soup with shells

preparation time: about 40 minutes

8 cups low-sodium chicken broth

2 cups diced carrots

4 ounces (about 1 cup) dried small shell-shaped pasta

2 cups thinly sliced asparagus

1 package (about 10 oz.) frozen tiny peas

1 ¼ to 1 ½ pounds tiny cooked shrimp.

½ cup thinly sliced green onions

¼ cup minced parsley

Parsley sprigs (optional)

Salt and pepper

1 Bring broth to a boil in a 5- to 6-quart pan over high heat. Stir in carrots and pasta; reduce heat, cover, and boil gently just until carrots and pasta are tender to bite 8 to 10 minutes; or according to package directions).

2 Add asparagus and peas; cook until heated through (about 2 minutes). Remove from heat and keep warm.

3 Combine shrimp, onions, and minced parsley in a small bowl. Ladle soup into bowls and spoon in shrimp mixture, dividing evenly. Garnish with parsley sprigs, if desired. Offer salt and pepper to add to taste.

makes 8 to 10 servings

per serving: 178 calories, 22 g protein, 18 g carbohydrates, 3 g total fat, 136 mg cholesterol, 312 mg sodium

pozole

preparation time: about 2 hours

1 pound pork tenderloin, trimmed of fat and silvery membrane and cut into 1 1/2-inch chunks

1 pound skinless, boneless chicken or turkey thighs, cut into 1 1/2-inch chunks

3 quarts low-sodium chicken broth

2 large onions, cut unto chunks

1 teaspoon dry oregano

1/2 teaspoon cumin seeds

2 cans (about 14 oz. *each*) yellow hominy, drained

Salt and pepper

Lime slices or wedges

1 1/2 cups crisp corn tortilla strips

1 Place pork and chicken in a 6- to 8-quart pan. Add broth, onions, oregano, and cumin seeds to pan. Bring to a boil over high heat; then reduce heat, cover, and simmer until meat is tender when pierced (about 1 1/2 hours). Lift out meat with a slotted spoors; place in a bowl to cool.

2 Pour cooking broth into a strainer set over a bowl. Press residue to remove liquid; discard residue. Return broth to pan and bring to a boil over high heat.

3 Add hominy and reduce heat; simmer, uncovered, until flavors are blended (about 10 minutes). Coarsely shred meat and return to broth. Serve soup hot or warm. If made ahead, let cool; then cover and refrigerate until next day. Reheat before serving.

4 To serve, ladle into bowls. Season to taste with salt and pepper and serve with lime slices and tortilla strips.

makes 8 to 10 servings

per serving: 265 calories, 27 g protein, 25 g carbohydrates, 8 g total fat. 75 mg cholesterol. 429 mg sodium

golden tomato-papaya gazpacho

preparation time: 20 minutes
chilling time: at least 2 hours

2 pounds ripe yellow regular or cherry tomatoes

1 large ripe papaya, peeled, seeded, and diced

1 cup diced cucumber

1/4 cup minced onion

2 tablespoons white wine vinegar

2 cups low sodium chicken broth

2 tablespoons minced fresh basil

1/8 teaspoon liquid hot pepper seasoning

Salt

Basil sprigs

1 Dice tomatoes; place in a large nonmetal bowl. Stir in papaya, cucumber, onion, vinegar, broth, minced basil, and hot pepper seasoning. Season to taste with salt.

2 Cover and refrigerate until cold (at least 2 hours) or until next day. Garnish with basil sprigs.

makes 10 to 12 servings

per serving: 37 calories, 2 g protein, 8 g carbohydrates, 0.7 g total fat, 0 mg cholesterol, 30 mg sodium

sherried lentil bisque

preparation time: about 1 1/2 hours

2 packages (about 12 oz. *each*, about 3 1/2 cups *total*) lentils

11 cups vegetable broth

3 cups chopped celery

3 cups chopped carrots

3 large onions, chopped

1 small red or green bell pepper, seeded and finely chopped

1 medium-size zucchini, finely chopped

3 tablespoons dry sherry

4 1/2 teaspoons cream sherry

1 cup reduced-fat sour cream

Thinly sliced green onions

Salt and pepper

1 Sort through lentils, discarding any debris. Rinse and drain lentils; place in an 8- to 10-quart pan and add broth, celery, carrots, chopped onions, bell pepper, and zucchini. Bring to a boil over high heat; then reduce heat, cover, and simmer until lentils are very soft to bite (about 50 minutes).

2 In a food processor or blender, whirl hot lentil mixture, a portion at a time, until smoothly puréed. Return purée to pan and stir in dry sherry and cream sherry. If made ahead, let cool; then cover and refrigerate until next day.

3 To serve, stir soup often aver medium-high heat until steaming; ladle into bowls. Top with sour cream and green onions; season to taste with salt and pepper.

makes 12 servings

per servings: 293 calories, 19 g protein, 47 g carbohydrates, 4 g total fat, 7 mg cholesterol, 959 mg sodium

mexican beef & pork birria

preparation time: about 2 1/2 hours

1 pound boneless beef top round, trimmed of fat

1/2 pound lean boneless pork, trimmed of fat

1 medium-size onion, thinly sliced

1 medium-size carrot, coarsely shredded

2 cloves garlic, minced or pressed

3 tablespoons chili powder

1 teaspoon *each* ground cumin and salad oil

4 cups water

2 cans (14 1/2 oz. *each*) regular-strength beef broth

Salt

About 1/2 cup sliced green onions (including tops)

1 large lime, cut into 6 wedges

1 Cut beef and pork into 1-inch cubes. In a 3 1/2- to 4-quart pan, combine meat with onion, carrot, garlic, chili powder, cumin, oil, and 1/2 cup of the water. Cover and simmer over medium-low heat for 30 minutes.

2 Uncover; increase heat to medium and cook, stirring often, until liquid has evaporated (20 to 25 minutes). Add 1 cup more of the water, stirring to loosen any browned bits in pan. Blend in remaining 2 1/2 cups water and beef broth. Bring to a boil; then cover, reduce heat, and simmer until meat is very tender (about 1 1/2 hours). Skim and discard surface fat, if necessary. Season to taste with salt. Garnish with green onions and lime.

makes 6 servings

per serving: 207 calories, 28 g protein, 7 g carbohydrates, 36 g total fat, 67 mg cholesterol, 608 mg sodium

green & white spring soup

preparation time: 20 minutes

1 large can (about 49½ oz.) fat-free
   reduced-sodium chicken broth

1 can (about 14½ oz.) fat-free
   reduced-sodium chicken broth

1 teaspoon grated lemon peel

1 teaspoon dried tarragon

¼ teaspoon white pepper

2 ounces dried capellini (angel hair pasta),
   broken in half

1 pound slender asparagus

12 ounces bay or sea scallops

1 bunch watercress

3 tablespoons lemon juice

1 In a 5- to 6-quart pan, combine broth, lemon peel, tarragon, and pepper. Bring to a boil over high heat. Add pasta; return broth to a boil, then reduce heat and simmer, uncovered, for 4 minutes.

2 Meanwhile, snap off and discard tough ends of asparagus; diagonally slice spears into 1-inch pieces. Rinse scallops; if using sea scallops, cut into bite-size pieces. Remove leaves from watercress; discard stems. Rinse and drain watercress. Chiffonade-cut 12 watercress leaves and set aside for garnish.

3 Stir asparagus and scallops into soup. Simmer, uncovered, until scallops are just opaque in center; cut to test (about 3 minutes).

4 Remove pan from heat and stir in whole watercress leaves. Cover and let stand until watercress is wilted (about 1 minute). Stir in lemon juice and sprinkle with the chiffonade of watercress. Serve immediately, since lemon juice may cause the bright green color to darken upon standing.

makes 5 servings (about 10 cups)

per serving: 147 calories, 20 g protein, 14 g carbohydrates, 1 g total fat, 22 mg cholesterol, 990 mg sodium

mexi-corn cheese soup

preparation time: 15 minutes

2 tablespoons butter or margarine

1 medium-size onion, finely chopped

½ teaspoon ground cumin

1 tablespoon cornstarch

2 cans (about 14½ oz. *each*) fat-free
   reduced-sodium chicken broth

1 package (about 10 oz.) frozen corn kernels

1 jar (about 7 oz.) roasted red peppers,
   drained and chopped

¼ cup salsa

8 ounces jalapeño jack cheese

1 Melt butter in a 3- to 4-quart pan over medium-high heat. Add onion and cumin; cook, stirring often, until onion is soft (4 to 5 minutes).

2 In a cup, dissolve cornstarch in about ¼ cup of the broth. Stir broth mixture into onion mixture in pan. Blend in remaining broth, corn, roasted peppers, and salsa. Bring to a boil over high heat, stirring occasionally; then reduce heat to a simmer and cook, stirring often, until soup thickens slightly.

3 Meanwhile, shred cheese. Just before serving, sprinkle soup with cheese.

makes 4 servings (about 6 cups)

per serving: 399 calories, 20 g protein, 28 g carbohydrates, 24 g total fat, 76 mg cholesterol, 1,199 mg sodium

curried fish chowder

preparation time: about 50 minutes

1 tablespoon margarine

1 large onion, chopped

2 tablespoons minced fresh ginger

1 clove garlic, minced or pressed

1 1/2 tablespoons curry powder

6 cups regular-strength chicken broth or chicken-vegetable stock

1 pound thin-skinned potatoes, unpeeled, cut into 1/2-inch cubes

1/2 pound carrots, cut into 1/2-inch cubes

3 strips (*each* 1/2 by 4 inches) lemon peel (yellow part only)

2 small dried hot red chiles

1 pound rockfish fillets, cut into 1/2-inch cubes

1/4 cup thinly sliced green onions (including tops)

1 cup nonfat plain yogurt

1 lemon, cut into wedges

1 Melt margarine in a 5- to 6-quart pan over medium-high heat. Add chopped onion, ginger, and garlic; cook, stirring occasionally, until onion is soft (about 7 minutes). Add curry powder; stir for 2 minutes. Add broth, potatoes, carrots, lemon peel, and chiles; bring to a boil over high heat. Reduce heat, cover, and simmer until potatoes are tender when pierced (about 20 minutes).

2 Add fish. Cover and simmer until fish is opaque (about 2 minutes). If desired, remove and discard chiles. Ladle soup into a tureen and sprinkle with green onions; top with yogurt. Serve with lemon wedges.

makes 4 to 6 servings

per serving: 246 calories, 21 g protein, 28 g carbohydrates, 6 g total fat, 29 mg cholesterol, 1,120 mg sodium

sausage-barley soup with swiss chard

preparation time: about 1 1/2 hours

1 pound turkey kielbasa, cut into 1/4-inch-thick slices

1 large onion, chopped

2 large carrots, thinly sliced

10 cups beef broth

1 cup pearl barley, rinsed and drained

1 tablespoon minced fresh oregano or 1 teaspoon dry oregano

8 ounces Swiss chard

Prepared horseradish and Dijon mustard

1 In a 5- to 6-quart pan, combine sausage, onion, and carrots. Cook over medium heat, stirring often, until sausage and vegetables are lightly browned (about 15 minutes). Discard any fat from pan.

2 To pan, add broth, barley, and oregano. Bring to a boil; then reduce heat, cover, and simmer until barley is tender to bite— about 30 minutes. (At this point, you may let cool, then cover and refrigerate for up to 1 day. Reheat before continuing.)

3 Trim and discard stem ends from chard; rinse chard well, then coarsely chop and stir into soup. Simmer, uncovered, until chard stems are tender-crisp to bite (6 to 8 minutes). Serve soup with horseradish and mustard to add to taste.

makes 6 servings

per serving: 298 calories, 21 g protein, 37 g carbohydrates, 8 g total fat, 52 mg cholesterol, 2,134 mg sodium

black & white bean soup

preparation time: about 45 minutes

1 large onion, chopped

1 clove garlic, peeled and sliced

3 1/2 cups vegetable broth

1/3 cup oil-packed dried tomatoes, drained and finely chopped

4 green onions, thinly sliced

1/4 cup dry sherry

2 cans (about 15 oz. *each*) black beans, drained and rinsed well

2 cans (about 15 oz. *each*) cannellini (white kidney beans), drained and rinsed

Slivered green onions (optional)

1 In a 5- to 6-quart pan, combine chopped onion, garlic, and 1/2 cup water. Cook over medium-high heat, stirring often, until liquid evaporates and browned bits stick to pan bottom (about 10 minutes). To deglaze pan, add 2 tablespoons of the broth, stirring to loosen browned bits from pan; continue to cook until browned bits form again. Repeat deglazing step, using 2 tablespoons more broth. Then stir in 1/2 cup more broth and pour mixture into a food processor or blender.

2 In same pan, combine tomatoes and sliced green onions. Cook over high heat, stirring, until onions are wilted (about 2 minutes). Add sherry and stir until liquid has evaporated. Remove from heat.

3 To onion mixture in food processor, add black beans. Whirl, gradually adding 1 1/4 cups of the broth, until smoothly puréed. Pour into a 3- to 4-quart pan.

4 Rinse processor; add cannellini and whirl until smoothly puréed, gradually adding remaining 1 1/2 cups broth. Stir puréed cannellini into pan with tomato mixture. Place both pans of soup over medium-high heat and cook, stirring often, until steaming.

5 To serve, pour soup into 6 wide 1 1/2- to 2-cup bowls as follows. From pans (or from 2 lipped containers such as 4-cup pitchers, which are easier to handle), pour soups simultaneously into opposite sides of each bowl so that soups flow together but do not mix. Garnish with slivered green onions, if desired.

makes 6 servings

per serving: 283 calories, 14 g protein, 38 g carbohydrates, 8 g total fat, 0 mg cholesterol, 996 mg sodium

lunchbox vegetable soup

preparation time: 30 minutes

4 large carrots

1 tablespoon butter or margarine

3 stalks celery, cut into ½-inch squares

1 large onion, chopped

1½ cups sliced mushrooms

1 can (about 15 oz.) baby corn on the cob, drained

1 large can (about 49½ oz.) fat-free reduced-sodium chicken broth

1 can (about 14½ oz.) fat-free reduced-sodium chicken broth

1½ teaspoons dried tarragon

¼ teaspoon pepper

Salt

2 cups dried pasta bow ties

1 cup frozen tiny peas

¼ cup chopped parsley

1 Peel carrots and cut crosswise into thin rounds.

2 Melt butter in a 5- to 6-quart pan over medium-high heat. Add carrots, celery, onion, mushrooms, and corn. Cook, stirring often, until celery and onion are tender to bite (5 to 6 minutes).

3 Add broth, tarragon, pepper, and salt to taste (about ¼ teaspoon); bring to a boil. Stir in pasta; return to a boil and cook, uncovered, for 5 minutes.

4 Add peas and continue to cook, uncovered, until pasta is just tender to bite (7 to 8 more minutes). Sprinkle with parsley.

makes 6 servings (about 12 cups)

per serving: 159 calories, 9 g protein, 25 g carbohydrates, 3 g total fat, 5 mg cholesterol, 846 mg sodium

spring shrimp soup

preparation time: 25 minutes

1 large can (about 49½ oz.) fat-free reduced-sodium chicken broth

1 pound peeled baby-cut carrots, cut in half lengthwise

12 ounces slender asparagus

4 green onions

1 package (about 10 oz.) frozen tiny peas

1 pound small cooked shrimp

¼ cup minced parsley

1 In a 5- to 6-quart pan, combine broth and carrots. Bring to a boil over high heat. Boil, uncovered, until carrots are almost tender to bite (5 to 6 minutes).

2 Meanwhile, snap off and discard tough ends of asparagus; diagonally slice spears ¼ inch thick. Thinly slice onions and set aside.

3 Add asparagus and peas to broth mixture; simmer just until asparagus is tender to bite (2 to 3 minutes).

4 Add onions, shrimp, and parsley; cook until shrimp are heated through (2 to 3 minutes).

makes 5 servings (about 10 cups)

per serving: 202 calories, 28 g protein, 19 g carbohydrates, 2 g total fat, 177 mg cholesterol, 982 mg sodium

hot & sour tofu soup

preparation time: 55 minutes

8 medium-size dried shiitake mushrooms

1 teaspoons salad oil

1 clove garlic, minced or pressed

1 tablespoon minced fresh ginger

10 cups fat-free reduced-sodium chicken broth

4 ounces dried linguine, broken into 3-inch pieces

1 pound regular reduced-fat tofu, rinsed and drained, cut into 1/2-inch cubes

3 tablespoons seasoned rice vinegar; or 3 tablespoons distilled white vinegar and 2 teaspoons sugar (or to taste)

5 teaspoons reduced-sodium soy sauce (or to taste)

3 tablespoons cornstarch mixed with 1/4 cup water

4 green onions, thinly sliced

Chili oil

1 Soak mushrooms in boiling water to cover until soft (about 20 minutes). Drain; cut off and discard coarse stems. Cut caps into thin strips; Set aside.

2 Heat salad oil in a 5- to 6-quart pan over medium heat. Add garlic and ginger. Cook, stirring, until garlic is light golden (about 2 minutes); if pan appears dry or garlic sticks to pan bottom, stir in water, 1 tablespoon (15 ml) at a time. Add broth and mushrooms; bring to a boil over high heat. Stir in pasta; reduce heat, cover, and boil gently just until pasta is tender to bite (8 to 10 minutes; or according to package directions).

3 Add tofu, vinegar, and soy sauce. Stir cornstarch mixture; add to soup, stirring until smooth. Cook over medium-high heat, stirring, just until soup comes to a boil and thickens slightly. Add onions; ladle into bowls. offer chili oil to add to taste.

makes 6 to 8 servings

per serving: 151 calories, 12 g protein, 22 g carbohydrates, 2 g total fat, 0 mg cholesterol, 1,248 mg sodium

cantaloupe-tangerine soup

preparation time: about 10 minutes

1 large cantaloupe, chilled

1 small can (about 6 oz.) frozen tangerine or orange juice concentrate, partially thawed

Mint sprigs

1 Cut cantaloupe in half; scoop out and discard seeds. Scoop fruit from rind and place in a food processor or blender; add tangerine juice concentrate and whirl until smoothly puréed. If made ahead, cover and refrigerate for up to 1 day; whirl again to blend before serving.

2 To serve, pour soup into bowls and garnish with mint sprigs.

makes 4 servings

per serving: 146 calories, 2 g protein, 35 g carbohydrates, 0.7 g total fat, 0 mg cholesterol, 17 mg sodium

tomato fava soup

preparation time: 55 minutes

2 tablespoons olive oil

1 large onion, chopped

1 1/2 pounds ripe tomatoes, quartered

2 tablespoons finely chopped fresh savory or
   1 teaspoon dried savory

3/4 teaspoon sugar

1/4 teaspoon pepper

2 cups shelled fava beans; see Note

4 cups fat-free reduced-sodium chicken broth

1 Heat oil in a 3- to 4-quart pan over medium-high heat. Add onion and cook, stirring often, until it begins to brown (5 to 10 minutes). Add tomatoes, savory, sugar, and pepper. Bring to a boil; then reduce heat and simmer, uncovered, until tomatoes are very soft when pressed (about 15 minutes).

2 Meanwhile, in a 2- to 3-quart pan, bring 4 cups water to a boil over high heat. Add beans and simmer, uncovered, until just tender when pierced (3 to 5 minutes). Drain, then let stand until cool enough to touch. With your fingers, slip skins from beans; discard skins and set beans aside.

3 In a food processor or blender, whirl tomato mixture until coarsely puréed. Return to pan and add broth; stir over high heat until hot. Ladle soup into individual bowls; sprinkle beans equally over each serving.

makes 6 servings

per serving: 261 calories, 17 g protein, 39 g carbohydrates, 6 g total fat, 0 mg cholesterol, 447 mg sodium

Note: A few people, typically of Mediterranean descent, have a severe allergic reaction to fava beans and their pollen. If favas are new to you, check your family history before eating them.

warm-up vegetable soup

preparation time: about 1 hour

1 tablespoon olive oil or salad oil

1 medium-size onion, finely chopped

8 ounces mushrooms, thinly sliced

1 teaspoon *each* dry oregano, dry basil, and
   dry marjoram

6 cups low-sodium chicken broth

1 medium-size thin-skinned potato, peeled and
   cut into 1/2-inch cubes

1 pound banana squash, peeled and cut into
   1/2-inch cubes

3/4 cup dry small shell-shaped pasta

1 cup diced pear-shaped (Roma-type) tomatoes

Salt and pepper

1 Heat oil in a 5- to 6-quart pan over medium heat. Add onion, mushrooms, oregano, basil, and marjoram. Cook, stirring often, until vegetables are tinged with brown (about 10 minutes). Stir in broth, potato, and squash. Bring to a boil; reduce heat, cover, and boil gently until potato is tender to bite (about 15 minutes).

2 Add pasta, cover, and continue to cook until pasta is just tender to bite (10 to 12 minutes). Stir in tomatoes; simmer until heated through (about 2 minutes). Season to taste with salt and pepper.

makes 6 servings

per serving: 171 calories, 7 g protein, 27 g carbohydrates, 5 g total fat, 0 mg cholesterol, 65 mg sodium

ravioli & cabbage soup

preparation time: about 40 to 55 minutes

4 ounces sliced bacon (about 5 slices),
  cut into ½-inch pieces

1 small onion, finely chopped

2 cloves garlic, minced or pressed

1 tablespoon chopped parsley

2 quarts regular-strength beef broth

2 cups water

1 large carrot, thinly sliced

1 pound (about 24) fresh or frozen ravioli;
  or 1 package (7 oz.) dry raviolini

2 cups shredded cabbage

Grated Parmesan cheese

1 In a 5- to 6-quart pan, cook bacon over medium heat until translucent and limp. Add onion; continue to cook, stirring, until onion and bacon are lightly browned (about 5 more minutes). Discard all but 1 tablespoon of the bacon drippings; then stir garlic and parsley into bacon-onion mixture. Add broth, water, and carrot. Increase heat to high and bring to a boil. Separate any ravioli that are stuck together, then add ravioli to boiling broth.

2 Reduce heat to medium and boil gently, uncovered, stirring occasionally, until ravioli are just tender to bite (about 10 minutes for fresh, 12 minutes for frozen, or 25 minutes for dry; or time according to package directions). Stir in cabbage during last 5 minutes of cooking. Serve with cheese to add to taste.

makes 4 to 6 servings

per serving: 473 calories, 20 g protein, 33 g carbohydrates, 28 g total fat, 90 mg cholesterol, 1,945 mg sodium

chinese chicken & shrimp soup

preparation time: about 20 minutes

5 cups regular-strength chicken broth

2 tablespoons finely chopped fresh ginger

2 to 3 teaspoons soy sauce

1 whole chicken breast (about 1 lb.), skinned,
  boned, and cut into ½-inch cubes

6 ounces mushrooms, sliced

3 cups thinly sliced bok choy

1 cup cubed firm tofu (about ½-inch cubes)

½ cup sliced green onions (including tops)

½ pound small cooked shrimp

¼ cup chopped fresh cilantro

Ground red pepper (cayenne) or chili oil
  (optional)

In a 4- to 5-quart pan, bring broth, ginger, and soy sauce to a boil over high heat. Add chicken, mushrooms, bok choy, tofu, and onions. Cook until chicken is no longer pink in center; cut to test (about 2 minutes). Remove pan from heat and stir in shrimp and cilantro. Season to taste with red pepper, if desired.

makes 4 to 6 servings

per serving: 230 calories, 36 g protein, 7 g carbohydrates, 7 g total fat, 123 mg cholesterol, 1,335 mg sodium

cinnamon-spice acorn soup

preparation time: 15 minutes

1 large onion, cut into chunks

2 packages (about 10 oz. *each*) frozen mashed squash, thawed

2 cans (about 14½ oz. *each*) fat-free reduced-sodium chicken broth

¼ teaspoon ground cinnamon

¼ teaspoon freshly grated or ground nutmeg

2 tablespoons butter or margarine

¼ cup sour cream and additional ground cinnamon (optional)

1 In a food processor or blender, whirl onion until puréed. Add squash, broth, the ¼ teaspoon cinnamon, and nutmeg; whirl until blended.

2 Pour squash mixture into a 3- to 4-quart pan. Bring to a simmer over medium-high heat, stirring occasionally; then continue to simmer, uncovered, until heated through (2 to 3 more minutes).

3 Add butter and stir until melted. If desired, season sour cream lightly with cinnamon and swirl on top of soup.

makes 4 servings (about 8 cups)

per serving: 167 calories, 6 g protein, 25 g carbohydrates, 6 g total fat, 16 mg cholesterol, 554 mg sodium

spring vegetable soup

preparation time: about 40 minutes

8 cups fat-free reduced sodium chicken broth

2 cups diced carrots

4 ounces dried small shell-shaped pasta

2 cups thinly sliced asparagus

1 package (about 10 oz.) frozen tiny peas

1¼ to 1½ pounds tiny cooked shrimp

½ cup thinly sliced green onions

¼ cup minced parsley

Parsley sprigs (optional)

Salt and pepper

1 Bring broth to a boil in a 5-to 6-quart pan over high heat. Stir in carrots and pasta; reduce heat, cover, and boil gently just until carrots and pasta are tender to bite (8 to 10 minutes; or according to package directions).

2 Add asparagus and peas; cook until heated through (about 2 minutes). Remove from heat and keep warm.

3 Combine shrimp, onions, and minced parsley in a small bowl. Ladle soup into bowls and spoon in shrimp mixture. Garnish with parsley sprigs, if desired. Offer salt and pepper to add to taste.

makes 8 to 10 servings

per serving: 178 calories, 22 g protein, 18 g carbohydrates, 3 g total fat, 136 mg cholesterol, 312 mg sodium

curried zucchini soup

preparation time: 25 minutes

3 slices bacon

7 large zucchini

8 green onions

1 large can (about 49½ oz.) fat-free reduced-sodium chicken broth

1 to 1¼ teaspoons curry powder

Salt

¼ teaspoon white pepper

¾ cup whipping cream

1 In a 4- to 5-quart pan, cook bacon over medium-high heat until crisp (5 to 6 minutes). Lift bacon from pan; drain, crumble, and set aside. Discard all but 1 tablespoon of the drippings from pan.

2 While bacon is cooling, coarsely chop zucchini. Chop onions and reserve 2 tablespoons for garnish.

3 To drippings in pan, add remaining onions, zucchini, broth, curry powder, salt to taste (about ¼ teaspoon), and pepper. Bring to a boil over high heat; then boil, uncovered, until zucchini mashes easily with a spoon (9 to 10 minutes).

4 In a food processor or blender, whirl zucchini mixture, half at a time, until smoothly puréed. Return to pan and stir in cream; reheat until steaming (do not boil). Serve hot or cold; garnish with bacon and reserved onions.

makes 4 servings (about 8 cups)

per serving: 281 calories, 13 g protein, 16 g carbohydrates, 20 g total fat, 57 mg cholesterol, 983 mg sodium

reuben soup pot with dijon toast

preparation time: 30 minutes

8 ounces fresh sauerkraut

8 ounces thinly sliced corned beef

1 large can (about 49½ oz.) fat-free reduced-sodium chicken broth

1 teaspoon caraway seeds

1 small ripe tomato

2 green onions

Dijon Toast (below)

1 cup shredded Swiss cheese

DIJON TOAST:

4 slices rye or pumpernickel bread

3 tablespoons Dijon mustard

¾ cup shredded Swiss cheese

Caraway seeds

1 Rinse and drain sauerkraut in a colander. Cut corned beef into thin strips.

2 In a 5- to 6-quart pan, bring broth, sauerkraut, and the 1 teaspoon caraway seeds to a boil. Add beef and cook, uncovered, until heated through (4 to 5 minutes).

3 Meanwhile, chop tomato and thinly slice onions. Also prepare Dijon Toast.

4 To serve, remove soup from heat and stir in tomato. Ladle soup into soup plates and sprinkle with the 1 cup cheese. Top each serving with a slice of Dijon Toast and sprinkle with onions.

DIJON TOAST

Arrange bread on a baking sheet. Broil 4 to 6 inches below heat, turning once, until lightly browned on both sides (about 1 minute). Spread mustard evenly over one side of each toast slice; sprinkle toast evenly with the ¾ cup cheese, then sprinkle with a few caraway seeds. Return to broiler until cheese is melted (about 30 seconds).

makes 4 servings (about 7 cups)

per serving: 460 calories, 32 g protein, 20 g carbohydrates, 25 g total fat, 101 mg cholesterol, 2,421 mg sodium

balkan prosciutto soup

preparation time: 30 minutes

1 tablespoon butter or margarine

2 large shallots, chopped

1 large can (about 49 ½ oz.) fat-free reduced-sodium chicken broth

½ teaspoon pepper

¼ teaspoon ground nutmeg

1 cup dried pastina (tiny pasta for soup)

4 cups packaged triple-washed spinach

2 ounces prosciutto, cut into thin strips

1 cup sour cream

1 Melt butter in a 4- to 5-quart pan over medium-high heat. Add shallots and cook, stirring often, until soft (about 5 minutes).

2 Stir in broth, pepper, and nutmeg. Bring to a boil; then add pastina. Reduce heat and simmer, uncovered, until pastina is just tender to bite (8 to 9 minutes).

3 Meanwhile, remove and discard any coarse stems from spinach. Stir spinach and prosciutto into soup; cook until prosciutto is heated through and spinach is wilted (4 to 5 minutes).

4 Remove from heat and smoothly blend in sour cream.

makes 4 servings (about 8 cups)

per serving: 367 calories, 17 g protein, 35 g carbohydrates, 18 g total fat, 45 mg cholesterol, 1,204 mg sodium

puget sound oyster stew

preparation time: 40 to 45 minutes

¼ cup butter or margarine

1 large onion, chopped

½ cup chopped parsley or 2 tablespoons parsley flakes

1 large green bell pepper, stemmed, seeded, and chopped

4 cups homemade chicken broth or 2 cans (14½ oz. *each*) regular-strength chicken broth

1 cup dry white wine

1 pound potatoes, peeled and cut into ¼-inch cubes (optional)

½ to 1 cup whipping cream

2 to 3 cups shucked raw oysters and juices (cut large oysters in bite-size pieces)

Salt and pepper

1 Melt butter in a 4- to 5-quart pan over medium-high heat. Add onion, parsley, and bell pepper. Cook, stirring often, until onion is soft, about 10 minutes. Stir in broth and wine, cover, and bring to a boil.

2 If using potatoes, add to boiling broth; reduce heat, cover, and simmer until potatoes mash easily, 10 to 15 minutes.

3 Add cream and oysters; simmer just until oysters are heated through, 1 to 2 minutes. Season to taste with salt and pepper.

makes 4 to 6 servings

per serving: 281 calories, 10 g protein, 15 g carbohydrates, 20 g total fat, 105 mg cholesterol, 173 mg sodium

chinese chicken stir-fry soup

preparation time: 30 minutes

1½ pounds boneless, skinless chicken breasts

8 green onions

2 tablespoons cornstarch

2 tablespoons reduced-sodium soy sauce

¼ teaspoon crushed red pepper flakes

1 medium-size head bok choy

1 large red bell pepper

1 large can (about 49½ oz.) fat-free reduced-sodium chicken broth

1 tablespoon vegetable oil

8 ounces sliced mushrooms

12 ounces shelled, deveined cooked shrimp (31 to 40 per lb.)

Fried Chinese chow mein noodles (optional)

1 Rinse chicken, pat dry, and cut into bite-size pieces. Diagonally slice onions into ½-inch lengths. On a large, shallow platter, toss together chicken, onions, cornstarch, soy sauce, and red pepper flakes. Cover and refrigerate for 5 minutes.

2 While chicken marinates, cut bok choy crosswise into ¼-inch-wide strips. Seed bell pepper and cut into thin strips.

3 In a 3-quart pan, bring broth to a simmer over medium-high heat. Meanwhile, heat oil in a 5- to 6-quart pan over high heat. Add chicken mixture, mushrooms, bok choy, and bell pepper to hot oil. Cook, stirring often, just until chicken is no longer pink in center; cut to test (5 to 6 minutes).

4 Add hot broth and shrimp to pan and cook, uncovered, until shrimp are heated through, (3 to 4 minutes). Mound fried noodles in center of soup, if desired.

makes 5 servings (about 10 cups)

per serving: 326 calories, 54 g protein, 14 g carbohydrates, 6 g total fat, 212 mg cholesterol, 1,262 mg sodium

cold cucumber & dill soup

preparation time: about 15 minutes

2 large cucumbers, peeled

1 cup regular-strength chicken broth

1 cup plain yogurt

¼ cup lightly packed chopped fresh dill

3 tablespoons lime juice

Salt

½ pound small cooked shrimp

Dill sprigs (optional)

1 Cut cucumbers into ½-inch chunks. Place half the cucumber chunks in a blender or food processor, add ½ cup of the broth, and whirl until puréed. Pour into a large bowl. Place remaining cucumbers, remaining ½ cup broth, yogurt, chopped dill, and lime juice in blender; whirl until puréed. Pour into bowl and stir to blend, then season to taste with salt. (For a smoother texture, rub soup through a fine sieve.)

2 Ladle soup into bowls and top with shrimp. Garnish each portion with dill sprigs, if desired.

makes 4 servings

per serving: 130 calories, 17 g protein, 11 g carbohydrates, 2 g total fat, 114 mg cholesterol, 428 mg sodium

shrimp drop soup

preparation time: 35 minutes

Shrimp Mixture (recipe follows)

1 large can (49½ oz.) regular-strength chicken broth

1 tablespoon soy sauce

1½ cups lightly packed shredded napa cabbage

⅓ cup frozen peas

1 Prepare Shrimp Mixture. In a 3- to 4-quart pan, bring broth to a boil over medium heat. Add soy sauce. Using 2 moistened teaspoons or a small melon-ball cutter to shape balls, drop ½-teaspoon portions of the shrimp mixture into boiling broth. As balls rise to surface, remove with a slotted spoon. (At this point, you may cover and refrigerate shrimp balls and broth separately until next day.)

2 Just before serving, return broth to a boil. Add cabbage, peas, and shrimp balls. Cook just until cabbage is bright green (1 to 2 minutes).

SHRIMP MIXTURE

Shell and devein ½ pound raw shrimp. In a food processor or blender, whirl shrimp until finely ground. Add 6 water chestnuts, chopped, 1 egg white, 2 teaspoons soy sauce, 1 teaspoon sesame oil, and a dash of pepper and whirl until blended.

makes 6 servings

per serving: 100 calories, 14 g protein, 7 g carbohydrates, 1 gram total fat, 71 mg cholesterol, 1156 mg sodium

shell & bean soup

preparation time: about 40 minutes

1 small red onion, chopped

1 teaspoon olive oil

1 cup chopped celery

4 cloves garlic, chopped

10 cups fat free reduced-sodium chicken broth

1½ cups dried small pasta shells

3 to 4 cups cooked or canned white beans, drained and rinsed

1 cup shredded carrots

1 package (about 10 oz.) frozen tiny peas

½ cup grated Parmesan cheese

1 Set aside ⅓ cup of the chopped onion. In a 6- to 8-quart pan, combine remaining onion, oil, celery and garlic. Cook over medium-high heat, stirring often, until onion is lightly browned (5 to 8 minutes). Add broth and bring to a boil. Stir in pasta and beans; reduce heat, cover, and simmer until pasta is almost tender to bite (5 to 7 minutes). Add carrots and peas; bring to a boil.

2 Ladle soup into individual bowls; sprinkle equally with cheese and reserved onion.

makes 6 to 8 servings

per serving: 324 calories, 22 g protein, 53 g carbohydrates, 3 g total fat. 5 mg cholesterol, 1,113 mg sodium

roasted pepper gazpacho

preparation time: 20 minutes

2 slices white Italian bread
(*each* about 2 inches thick)

6 large ripe pear-shaped
(Roma-type) tomatoes, chilled

2 medium-size cucumbers, chilled

1 large red onion, chilled

1 medium-size green bell pepper, chilled

3½ cups chilled tomato juice

1 cup cold water

1 jar (about 12 oz.) roasted red peppers,
chilled, drained

¼ cup red wine vinegar

2 tablespoons olive oil

2 cloves garlic, minced or pressed

Salt

½ teaspoon black pepper

¼ cup cilantro leaves

1 Remove crusts from bread; cut bread into 1-inch pieces. Set aside.

2 Seed and dice tomatoes. Peel, seed, and dice cucumbers. Chop onion; seed and dice bell pepper. Then, in a large bowl, toss together tomatoes, cucumbers, onion, and bell pepper.

3 In a food processor or blender, combine tomato juice, water, roasted peppers, bread, vinegar, oil, garlic, salt to taste (about ½ teaspoon), and black pepper. Whirl until mixture is almost smooth. Pour purée over vegetables in bowl; stir to combine.

4 Serve immediately; or cover and refrigerate for up to 3 days. Just before serving, chiffonade-cut cilantro and mound in a cluster in center of soup.

makes 4 servings (about 8 cups)

per serving: 250 calories, 6 g protein, 41 g carbohydrates, 8 g total fat, 0 mg cholesterol, 1,085 mg sodium

sicilian tomato soup

preparation time: 25 minutes

2 tablespoons olive oil

12 large ripe pear-shaped (Roma-type)
tomatoes, seeded and diced

24 large fresh basil leaves

¾ cup fat-free reduced-sodium chicken broth

¾ cup whipping cream

1 tablespoon Worcestershire sauce

Salt

¼ teaspoon crushed red pepper flakes

1 Heat oil in a 3- to 4-quart pan over medium-high heat. Add tomatoes and cook, stirring often, until tomatoes mash easily with a spoon (about 15 minutes).

2 Meanwhile, rinse basil leaves; drain on paper towels. Chiffonade-cut 8 of the leaves and set aside for garnish.

3 Transfer tomatoes to a food processor or blender. Add broth, cream, Worcestershire sauce, salt to taste (about ¼ teaspoon), red pepper flakes, and remaining 16 basil leaves. Whirl until almost smooth. Garnish with the chiffonade of basil.

makes 4 servings (about 4 cups)

per serving: 247 calories, 4 g protein, 12 g carbohydrates, 21 g total fat, 50 mg cholesterol, 321 mg sodium

chicken & vegetable soup

preparation time: 40 to 45 minutes

6 cups regular-strength chicken broth

½ cup long-grain white rice

3 medium-size carrots, cut into ⅛-inch-thick slices

3 stalks celery, cut into ¼-inch-thick slices

2 small zucchini, cut into ¼-inch-thick slices

6 tablespoons butter or margarine

6 tablespoons all-purpose flour

2 cups half-and-half or milk

3 cups bite-size pieces cooked chicken or turkey

½ cup thinly sliced green onions (including tops)

Salt and pepper

Minced parsley

1 In a 5-quart pan, bring broth to a boil over high heat. Add rice; reduce heat, cover, and simmer for 10 minutes. Add carrots, celery, and zucchini; cover and continue to simmer until vegetables are tender-crisp to bite (about 10 more minutes).

2 Meanwhile, melt butter in a small pan over medium heat. Stir in flour and cook, stirring, until bubbly. Remove from heat and gradually stir in half-and-half; then stir in about 1 cup of the broth from soup mixture. Return to heat and cook, stirring, until sauce is smooth and thickened. Stir sauce into soup mixture.

3 Stir in chicken and onions; season to taste with salt and pepper. Cook until heated through. Ladle into bowls and sprinkle with parsley.

makes 4 to 6 servings

per serving: 572 calories, 34 g protein, 34 g carbohydrates, 33 g total fat, 148 mg cholesterol, 1,475 mg sodium

sausage & kale soup

preparation time: about 40 minutes

1 pound linguiça sausage, cut diagonally into ¼-inch-thick slices

1 large onion, chopped

2 large carrots, chopped

10 cups regular-strength chicken broth

¾ pound kale, tough stems removed

Salt and pepper

1 In a 5- to 6-quart pan, cook sausage over high heat until browned (8 to 10 minutes), stirring. Discard all but 2 tablespoons of the drippings.

2 Add onion and carrots to drippings in pan and cook, stirring, until onion is soft (about 10 minutes). Add broth. Cover and bring to a boil.

3 Meanwhile, rinse and drain kale. Cut crosswise into ½-inch-wide strips. Add to boiling soup and cook, stirring, until limp and bright green (3 to 5 minutes). Season soup to taste with salt and pepper, then transfer to a large tureen or ladle into bowls.

makes 6 to 8 servings

per serving: 233 calories, 14 g protein, 11 g carbohydrates, 15 g total fat, 39 mg cholesterol, 1,649 mg sodium

autumn vegetable & turkey chowder

preparation time: about 45 minutes

3 tablespoons butter or margarine

1 medium-size onion, chopped

1 cup thinly sliced carrots

½ cup thinly sliced celery

2 cups diced potatoes

1 can (about 14½ oz.) tomatoes

2 beef bouillon cubes

1½ teaspoons Worcestershire

2 cups diced cooked turkey

2 cups milk

Salt and pepper

1½ cups shredded sharp Cheddar cheese

Chopped parsley

1 Melt butter in a 3-quart pan over medium heat. Add onion and cook, stirring, until soft (about 10 minutes). Stir in carrots, celery, potatoes, tomatoes (break up with a spoon) and their liquid, bouillon cubes, and Worcestershire. Bring to a boil; reduce heat, cover, and boil gently, stirring occasionally, until vegetables are tender to bite (about 15 minutes). Mix in turkey.

2 Gradually stir in milk; heat, stirring often, just until soup is steaming. Season to taste with salt and pepper; then add 1¼ cups of the cheese, stirring until cheese is melted. Ladle soup into bowls; sprinkle with parsley and remaining ¼ cup cheese.

makes 4 to 6 servings

per serving: 440 calories, 31 g protein, 25 g carbohydrates, 24 g total fat, 111 mg cholesterol, 870 mg sodium

fish pot-au-feu

preparation time: about 45 minutes

5 cups regular-strength chicken broth

1 cup dry white wine; or 1 cup regular-strength chicken broth and 3 tablespoons white wine vinegar

¼ teaspoon dry tarragon

4 small red thin-skinned potatoes, scrubbed

4 medium-size carrots, cut in half

4 medium-size leeks, roots and most of dark green tops trimmed

1½ pounds lean white-fleshed fish fillets, such as lingcod or sea bass

1 In a 5- to 6-quart pan, bring broth, wine, and tarragon to a boil over high heat. Add unpeeled potatoes and carrots and return to a boil; then reduce heat, cover, and boil gently for 10 minutes.

2 Meanwhile, split leeks lengthwise and rinse well. Add to pan, cover, and boil gently until leeks are tender when pierced (about 10 more minutes). Lift leeks from broth with a slotted spoon, cover, and keep warm.

3 Rinse fish and pat dry; cut into 4 equal portions. Add to soup, cover, and simmer just until vegetables are tender when pierced and fish is opaque but still moist in thickest part; cut to test (7 to 10 minutes).

4 With a slotted spatula, carefully lift fish from pan and arrange in 4 wide, shallow bowls. Evenly distribute vegetables alongside fish and ladle broth over all.

makes 4 servings

per serving: 349 calories, 37 g protein, 32 g carbohydrates, 4 g total fat, 89 mg cholesterol, 1,385 mg sodium

riviera fish soup

preparation time: 25 minutes

1 pound swordfish

8 ounces boneless, skinless salmon fillets

8 ounces sole fillets

1 tablespoon olive oil

2 stalks celery, finely chopped

1 large onion, thinly sliced

2 cloves garlic, minced or pressed

1 jar (about 26 oz.) fat-free, reduced-sodium extra-chunky pasta sauce with Italian-style vegetables

2 cups water

1/2 cup dry white wine

1/8 to 1/4 teaspoon crushed red pepper flakes

1/3 cup grated Parmesan cheese

1/3 cup slivered fresh basil or 2 tablespoons dried basil

1 Rinse all fish and pat dry. Cut fish into bite-size pieces and set aside.

2 Heat oil in a 5- to 6-quart pan over medium-high heat. Add celery, onion, and garlic; cook, stirring often, until celery is tender to bite (4 to 5 minutes).

3 Stir in pasta sauce, water, wine, and red pepper flakes. Bring to a boil. Then reduce heat, add fish, and simmer, uncovered, until fish is just opaque but still moist in thickest part; cut to test (5 to 6 minutes).

4 Remove pan from heat. Sprinkle soup with cheese and basil.

makes 6 servings (about 12 cups)

per serving: 296 calories, 34 g protein, 13 g carbohydrates, 10 g total fat, 72 mg cholesterol, 614 mg sodium

cabbage patch soup

preparation time: about 35 minutes

2 tablespoons butter or margarine

1 pound ground lean beef

1 medium-size onion, thinly sliced

1/2 cup thinly sliced celery

1 can (about 1 lb.) tomatoes

2 cups water

1 can (about 1 lb.) red kidney beans

1 teaspoon chili powder

1/8 teaspoon pepper

2 cups finely shredded green cabbage

Salt

1 Melt butter in a 10- to 12-inch frying pan or a 5- to 6-quart pan over medium heat. Add beef; cook, stirring, until browned and crumbly. Add onion and celery and stir often for about 5 minutes.

2 Stir in tomatoes (break up with a spoon) and their liquid, water, beans, chili powder, and pepper. Bring to a boil; add cabbage, reduce heat, cover, and simmer until cabbage is tender, about 5 minutes. Season to taste with salt.

makes 4 to 6 servings

per serving: 330 calories, 19 g protein, 18 g carbohydrates, 20 g total fat, 67 mg cholesterol, 482 mg sodium

mediterranean fish stew

preparation time: about 45 minutes

Spicy Hot Mayonnaise (recipe follows)

2 tablespoons salad oil

1 large onion, chopped

1 large green bell pepper, seeded and chopped

2 cloves garlic, minced or pressed

1 can (about 14½ oz.) pear-shaped tomatoes

1½ cups water

½ cup dry white wine or water

1 bottle (8 oz.) clam juice

3 chicken bouillon cubes

¼ teaspoon *each* dry basil, dry oregano, and dry thyme

2 pounds lean white-fleshed fish fillets, such as rockfish or lingcod

1 Prepare Spicy Hot Mayonnaise and set aside.

2 Heat oil in a 5- to 6-quart pan over medium heat. Add onion, bell pepper, and garlic; cook, stirring occasionally, until vegetables are soft (about 10 minutes). Add tomatoes (break up with a spoon) and their liquid, water, wine, clam juice, bouillon cubes, basil, oregano, and thyme. Stir until bouillon cubes are dissolved. Reduce heat, cover, and simmer for 15 minutes.

3 Rinse fish and pat dry; cut into 1-inch squares. Bring soup to a boil. Add fish, reduce heat, cover, and simmer just until fish is opaque but still moist in center; cut to test (6 to 8 minutes). Ladle into wide, shallow bowls. Pass mayonnaise to stir into individual servings

makes 4 to 6 servings

SPICY HOT MAYONNAISE

Mix ⅔ cup mayonnaise; 2 cloves garlic, minced or pressed; ¾ to 1 teaspoon ground red pepper (cayenne); 1 tablespoon white wine vinegar; and ¼ teaspoon salt. If made ahead, cover and refrigerate for up to 1 week.

makes about ⅔ cup

per serving of stew: 262 calories, 36 g protein, 9 g carbohydrates, 9 g total fat, 64 mg cholesterol, 1,026 mg sodium

per tablespoon of mayonnaise: 89 calories, 0.2 g protein, 0.6 g carbohydrates, 10 g total fat, 7 mg cholesterol, 115 mg sodium

mussel chowder

preparation time: about 50 minutes

2 quarts steamed mussels and their liquid

¼ cup butter or margarine

1 large onion, chopped

1 stalk celery, thinly sliced

½ pound button mushrooms, sliced

1 bay leaf

½ teaspoon paprika

2 cups homemade chicken broth or 1 can (14½ oz.) regular-strength chicken broth

1½ cups half-and-half or light cream

1 Remove mussels from shells; discard shells. Line a colander with moistened cheesecloth; pour mussel liquid through cloth. Measure liquid; you need 1½ cups (add water, if necessary). Set aside.

2 Melt butter in a 3- to 4-quart pan; add onion, celery, and mushrooms. Cook, stirring occasionally, until mushrooms are soft and lightly browned, 15 to 20 minutes. Add bay leaf, paprika, broth, and mussel liquid. Bring to a boil, then reduce heat, cover, and simmer for 15 minutes. Remove bay leaf. Stir in half-and-half and mussels, then cover and place over low heat just until hot; do not boil.

makes 4 to 6 servings

per serving: 252 calories, 13 g protein, 12 g carbohydrate, 17 g total fat, 77 mg cholesterol, 307 mg sodium

yaquina bay salmon chowder

preparation time: about 45 minutes

2 pounds salmon steaks or fillets
(*each* about 1 inch thick)

1 can (10¾ oz.) condensed chicken broth

1 bottle (8 oz.) clam juice

1 cup dry white wine

6 tablespoons butter or margarine

1 medium-size onion, chopped

2 stalks celery, chopped

¼ teaspoon *each* dry basil, dry thyme,
and dry marjoram

1½ cups milk

1 large can (about 28 oz.) tomatoes,
drained and chopped

1 tablespoon brandy

Salt and pepper

About 1½ cups shredded Cheddar cheese

1 Rinse salmon and pat dry. In a wide frying pan, combine broth, clam juice, and wine. Bring to a boil over high heat; reduce heat and place salmon in liquid. Cover and simmer until salmon is opaque but still moist in thickest part; cut to test (10 to 12 minutes). Lift out salmon and let cool slightly; then remove and discard bones, skin, and any gray-brown edges. Flake salmon and set aside; reserve poaching liquid.

2 Melt butter in a 4- to 5-quart pan over medium heat. Add onion and celery and cook, stirring, until onion is soft (about 10 minutes). Stir in basil, thyme, marjoram, milk, tomatoes, and poaching liquid. Cover and cook gently for 10 minutes. Add salmon, stir in brandy, and season to taste with salt and pepper. Ladle into bowls; offer cheese to add to individual portions.

makes 4 to 6 servings

per serving: 631 calories, 52 g protein, 13 g carbohydrates, 40 g total fat, 189 mg cholesterol, 1,228 mg sodium

venetian rice & peas in broth

preparation time: about 25 minutes

6 cups homemade chicken broth or 1 large can
(49½ oz.) regular-strength chicken broth

½ cup long-grain white rice

1 package (10 oz.) frozen tiny peas

Freshly grated Parmesan cheese (optional)

1 In a 3- to 4-quart pan, bring broth to a boil. Add rice; reduce heat, cover, and simmer until rice is tender, about 15 minutes. (At this point, you may cool, cover, and refrigerate until serving time.)

2 Return broth-rice mixture to a boil; stir in peas (first bang package sharply against a hard surface to separate peas). Simmer gently for 5 minutes. If desired, offer cheese to add to individual servings

makes 6 servings

per serving: 139 calories, 4 g protein, 26 g carbohydrates, 2 g total fat, 0 mg cholesterol, 70 mg sodium

mexican shellfish chowder

preparation time: 30 minutes

1 large can (about 49½ oz.) fat-free reduced-sodium chicken broth

1 can (about 14½ oz.) fat-free reduced-sodium chicken broth

½ cup dry white wine

1 can (about 14½ oz.) crushed tomatoes

⅓ cup medium-hot salsa

2 cloves garlic, minced or pressed

1 dried bay leaf

⅛ teaspoon ground saffron

24 small hard-shell clams in shell, scrubbed

8 ounces sea scallops

12 ounces shelled, deveined cooked shrimp (31 to 40 per lb.); leave tails on, if desired

3 tablespoons chopped cilantro

1 In a 5- to 6-quart pan, combine broth, wine, tomatoes and their liquid, salsa, garlic, bay leaf, and saffron. Bring to a boil over medium-high heat. Boil, uncovered, for 5 minutes.

2 Add clams; cover and simmer for 5 more minutes. Meanwhile, rinse scallops and cut crosswise into ½-inch-thick slices.

3 Add scallops and shrimp to pan. Cover and simmer until clams pop open and scallops are just opaque in center; cut to test (3 to 4 minutes). Remove pan from heat. Remove and discard bay leaf. Discard any unopened clams. Sprinkle soup with cilantro.

makes 6 servings (about 12 cups)

per serving: 161 calories, 26 g protein, 6 g carbohydrates, 1 g total fat, 121 mg cholesterol, 1,164 mg sodium

chicken barley soup

preparation time: about 55 minutes

1 tablespoon butter or margarine

1 large onion, thinly sliced and separated into rings

¼ cup pearl barley

⅛ teaspoon anise seeds, coarsely crushed

1 clove garlic, minced or pressed

6 cups regular-strength chicken broth

3 small carrots, sliced ¼ inch thick

1 medium-size orange

2 cups skinned and shredded cooked chicken or turkey

Chopped parsley

1 In a 3- to 4-quart pan, melt butter over medium heat. Add onion, barley, and anise seeds. Cook, stirring often, until onion is soft (6 to 8 minutes). Stir in garlic; then add broth. Reduce heat, cover, and boil gently until barley is almost tender to bite (about 25 minutes).

2 Add carrots, cover, and simmer until carrots are just tender (about 10 minutes).

3 Meanwhile, grate enough orange peel to make ¼ teaspoon; set aside. Cut off and discard remaining peel and white membrane from orange. Lift out orange segments and add to soup along with orange peel and chicken. Cover and simmer until chicken is heated through (3 to 5 minutes). Garnish with parsley.

makes 4 servings

per serving: 261 calories, 29 g protein, 23 g carbohydrates, 6 g total fat, 86 mg cholesterol, 1184 mg sodium

chicken, shiitake & bok choy soup

preparation time: about 1 hour

Ginger-Garlic Paste (recipe follows)

1½ tablespoons Asian sesame oil or salad oil

⅓ pound fresh shiitake or regular mushrooms, thinly sliced

8 green onions, sliced

3 cups low-sodium chicken broth

4 skinned, boned chicken breast halves (about 6 oz. *each*)

2 large carrots, cut into thin slanting slices

8 baby bok choy, coarse outer leaves removed

2 cups hot cooked short or medium-grain rice

3 tablespoons minced cilantro

1 Prepare Ginger-Garlic Paste and set aside.

2 Heat oil in a 4- to 5-quart pan over medium heat. Add mushrooms and half the onions; cook, stirring often, until mushrooms are lightly browned (about 10 minutes). Add broth and stir to loosen browned bits. Cover pan and bring broth to a boil over high heat.

3 Rinse chicken; pat dry. Add chicken and carrots to boiling broth, making sure they are covered with liquid. Reduce heat to low, cover pan tightly, and simmer until chicken is no longer pink in thickest part; cut to test (about 15 minutes).

4 Lift chicken to a cutting board. Add bok choy and remaining onions to pan; cover and simmer over medium heat until bok choy is bright green and just tender when pierced (about 5 minutes).

5 Meanwhile, cut chicken across the grain into inch-wide slanting slices.

6 Place a ½-cup scoop of rice off center in each of 4 wide, shallow soup bowls. Arrange a sliced chicken breast around each mound of rice. With a slotted spoon, distribute vegetables evenly among bowls. Stir cilantro into broth; gently pour into bowls over chicken and vegetables. Season each serving with about 2 tablespoons Ginger-Garlic Paste.

GINGER-GARLIC PASTE

In a blender or food processor, combine ¾ cup coarsely chopped fresh ginger, 3 cloves garlic, and 3 tablespoons seasoned rice vinegar (or 3 tablespoons distilled white vinegar plus 1 tablespoon sugar). Whirl until very smooth. If made ahead, cover and refrigerate for up to 4 hours.

makes 4 servings

per serving: 471 calories, 47 g protein, 49 g carbohydrates, 9 g total fat, 99 mg cholesterol, 230 mg sodium

turkey hot pot

preparation time: 45 minutes

2 ounces bean threads (cellophane noodles
  or long rice)

Turkey Meatballs (recipe follows)

2 medium-size carrots, cut diagonally
  into ⅛-inch slices

6 green onions (including tops),
  cut into 2-inch lengths

8 fresh shiitake or oyster mushrooms,
  cut in half if large

6 leaves napa cabbage, cut into 2-inch squares

4 cups regular-strength chicken broth

2 cups water

2 teaspoons soy sauce

1 Place bean threads in a bowl; cover with warm water and let soak for about 30 minutes. Prepare Turkey Meatballs and set aside. On a tray, arrange carrots, onions, mushrooms, and cabbage in separate piles.

2 In a 4- to 5-quart pan, combine broth, water, and soy sauce. Bring to a boil over high heat. Add meatballs, all at once. Return broth to a boil; reduce heat and simmer for 5 minutes. Skim and discard any foam or small particles that rise to surface.

3 Drain bean threads, discarding liquid. Without stirring, add to broth, in sequence, carrots, onions, mushrooms, cabbage, and bean threads, allowing broth to return to a simmer after each addition. (Try to keep each ingredient in its own area of pan for easier serving.)

4 Cover and simmer until vegetables are just tender when pierced (about 1 minute).

5 Distribute ingredients evenly among individual bowls, then ladle broth over.

makes 4 servings

TURKEY MEATBALLS

In a medium-size bowl, lightly mix 1 pound ground turkey, 1 teaspoon grated fresh ginger, 1 tablespoon cornstarch, 1 tablespoon sake or dry sherry, and ½ teaspoon salt. Add 1 egg, lightly beaten, and stir until blended. Shape into 1½-inch balls.

per serving: 331 calories, 42 g protein, 18 g carbohydrates, 9 g total fat, 178 mg cholesterol, 1395 mg sodium

mustard greens & millet soup

preparation time: 10 to 15 minutes
cooking time: 25 to 30 minutes;
30 to 35 minutes if eggs are used

10 cups homemade chicken broth
  or canned regular-strength chicken broth

2 cloves garlic, minced or pressed

½ cup millet

¾ pound mustard greens, tough stems
  trimmed off

4 to 6 large eggs (optional)

1 cup shredded jack cheese (optional)

1 In a 5- to 6-quart pan, bring broth, garlic, and millet to a boil over high heat. Reduce heat, cover, and simmer until millet is tender to bite, about 20 minutes.

2 Meanwhile, wash mustard greens well and pat dry. Stack leaves and cut crosswise into ½-inch strips. Stir mustard greens into broth; simmer, covered, for 5 minutes. Serve, or add eggs.

3 To add eggs, crack each egg into a bowl, then slide into soup; space eggs apart. Reduce heat slightly so soup does not bubble. Cover pan and cook until whites are set and yolks are soft or firm, as desired, 3 to 6 minutes.

4 Gently transfer eggs from pan to a tureen or individual bowls; ladle soup over eggs. Offer cheese to add to individual portions, if desired.

makes 4 to 6 servings

per serving: 147 calories, 4 g protein, 26 g carbohydrates, 4 g total fat, 0 mg cholesterol, 23 mg sodium

shrimp gumbo chowder

preparation time: 30 minutes

2 tablespoons vegetable oil

3 tablespoons all-purpose flour

1 large green bell pepper

3 slices bacon

1 package (about 10 oz.) frozen sliced okra

2 cloves garlic, minced or pressed

1 package (about 6 oz.) chicken-flavored rice
and vermicelli mix

1 large can (about 49½ oz.) fat-free
reduced-sodium chicken broth

1 large can (about 28 oz.) whole tomatoes
in purée

½ cup water

1 teaspoon liquid hot pepper seasoning
(or to taste)

1 pound shelled, deveined cooked shrimp
(31 to 40 per lb.)

1 Heat oil in a small frying pan over medium heat. Add flour and cook, stirring occasionally, until browned (4 to 5 minutes). Set aside.

2 While roux is cooking, seed and dice bell pepper; also dice bacon. Place bell pepper and bacon in a 5- to 6-quart pan; add okra and garlic. Cook over medium-high heat, stirring often, until bacon is translucent and vegetables begin to soften (4 to 5 minutes). Stir in roux and rice mix (rice and vermicelli plus seasoning packet).

3 Add broth, tomatoes and their purée, water, and hot pepper seasoning. Bring to a boil, stirring occasionally to break up tomatoes. Reduce heat, cover, and simmer until rice is tender to bite (8 to 10 minutes). Add shrimp to soup and cook until heated through.

makes 6 servings (about 12 cups)

per serving: 382 calories, 25 g protein, 38 g carbohydrates, 14 g total fat, 157 mg cholesterol, 1,554 mg sodium

fresh pea & pasta broth

preparation time: about 20 minutes

4 ounces sugar snap peas or Chinese pea pods
(also called snow or sugar peas), ends and
strings removed

1 large can (49½ oz.) regular-strength chicken
broth

2 whole star anise; or ¼ teaspoon crushed
anise seeds and 2 cinnamon sticks (each
2 inches long)

¾ teaspoon grated fresh ginger

1 ounce dry thin pasta, such as capellini
or coil vermicelli

1 Cut peas diagonally into ¼- to ½-inch-wide slices. Set aside.

2 In a 4- to 5-quart pan, combine broth, star anise, and ginger. Bring to a boil over high heat. Add pasta; return to a boil and cook, uncovered, just until pasta is tender to bite (about 3 minutes; or time according to package directions). Add peas; return to a boil. Remove whole spices, then serve soup immediately

makes 6 servings

per serving: 61 calories, 3 g protein, 8 g carbohydrates, 2 g total fat, 0 mg cholesterol, 1,036 mg sodium

TO MICROWAVE:

Cut peas as directed. In a 4-quart microwave-safe casserole or tureen, combine broth, star anise, and ginger. Microwave, covered, on HIGH (100%) for 12 to 15 minutes or until mixture comes to a boil. Add pasta; microwave, covered, on HIGH (100%) for 4 to 6 minutes or until pasta is almost tender to bite, stirring once. Add peas; microwave, covered, on HIGH (100%) for 2 minutes. Let stand, covered, for 2 minutes.

tomatillo fish stew

preparation time: about 40 minutes

1¼ pounds tomatillos, husked

1 fresh hot green or yellow chile (about 2½ inches long)

1 tablespoon olive oil or salad oil

1 small onion, finely chopped

1 cup corn cut from cob or thawed frozen corn

3 cups regular-strength chicken broth

½ cup slightly sweet white wine, such as Gewürztraminer or Chenin Blanc

1 pound boneless sea bass or other firm-textured white fish, such as lingcod or halibut, cut into bite-size pieces

½ cup chopped parsley

Nasturtium blossoms, well washed (optional)

1 Rinse and core tomatillos; thinly slice 3 of them and set aside. Chop remaining tomatillos. Thinly slice chile, discarding stem.

2 Heat oil in a 5- to 6-quart pan over medium-high heat; add chopped tomatillos, chile, onion, and corn. Cook, stirring occasionally, until mixture begins to brown on pan bottom (12 to 15 minutes). Add broth and wine; cover and bring to a boil over high heat. Add fish and sliced tomatillos. Remove from heat, cover, and let stand just until fish is opaque in center (1 to 2 minutes).

3 Serve hot, stirring in parsley before serving. Or let cool; cover, refrigerate until cold or until next day, and serve cold, adding parsley just before serving. Garnish with nasturtium blossoms, if desired.

makes 4 servings

per serving: 240 calories, 28 g protein, 21 g carbohydrates, 5 g total fat, 11 mg cholesterol, 632 mg sodium

crab & rice chowder

preparation tine: 45 to 50 minutes

1 tablespoon salad oil

1 small onion, finely chopped

8 ounces mushrooms, thinly sliced

½ teaspoon dry thyme

2 cups coarsely chopped broccoli flowerets

1 small red bell pepper, seeded and finely chopped

2 cups low-sodium chicken broth

2 cups lowfat milk

1 can (about 17 oz.) cream-style corn

6 ounces cooked crabmeat

3 cups cooked long-grain white rice

Salt and pepper

1 Heat oil in a 4- to 5-quart pan over medium-high heat. Add onion, mushrooms, and thyme; cook, stirring often, until vegetables begin to brown (about 8 minutes). Add broccoli and bell pepper; cook, stirring often, until broccoli turns bright green and begins to soften (about 4 minutes).

2 Stir in broth, milk, and corn; cook just until heated through, but do not boil (5 to 7 minutes). Stir in crab and rice; again, cook just until heated through (2 to 3 minutes). Season to taste with salt and pepper.

makes 6 servings

per serving: 327 calories, 15 g protein, 53 g carbohydrates, 6 g total fat, 35 mg cholesterol, 377 mg sodium

chicken-noodle yogurt soup

preparation time: about 1 hour

1 tablespoon salad oil

1 large onion, finely chopped

1 teaspoon thyme leaves

¼ teaspoon *each* pepper and dill weed

3 cloves garlic, minced or pressed

8 cups regular-strength chicken broth

4 or 5 parsley sprigs

3 small carrots, thinly sliced

4 ounces medium-wide egg noodles

2 cups skinned and cubed cooked chicken
   or turkey

1 cup plain lowfat yogurt

1 tablespoon cornstarch

6 green onions (including tops), thinly sliced

1 Heat oil in a 5- to 6-quart pan over medium heat; add chopped onion, thyme, pepper, and dill weed. Cook, stirring often, until onion is soft (6 to 8 minutes). Stir in garlic; then add broth, parsley, and carrots. Bring to a boil; reduce heat, cover, and boil gently until carrots are tender when pierced (12 to 15 minutes).

2 Discard parsley; increase heat to high and add noodles. Cook, uncovered, until noodles are tender (8 to 10 minutes). Add chicken.

3 In a medium-size bowl, smoothly blend yogurt and cornstarch. Gradually blend in about 1 cup of the hot broth mixture. Then stir yogurt mixture into soup and cook, stirring, until soup comes to a boil. Garnish with green onion slices.

makes 6 servings

per serving: 249 calories, 24 g protein, 25 g carbohydrates, 5 g total fat, 76 mg cholesterol, 1028 mg sodium

red onion borscht

preparation time: about 1 hour

1½ tablespoons salad oil

4 large red onions, thinly sliced

½ cup red wine vinegar

2 medium-size beets, peeled and shredded

2½ tablespoons all-purpose flour

6 cups low-sodium chicken broth

⅓ cup port

Salt and pepper

Light sour cream (optional)

1 Heat oil in a 5- to 6-quart pan over medium-low heat. Add onions, vinegar, and beets. Cook, stirring often, until onions are very soft but not browned (25 to 30 minutes). Add flour and stir until bubbly. Remove pan from heat and gradually stir in broth. (At this point, you may cover and refrigerate for up to 2 days.)

2 Return soup to medium heat and bring to a boil, stirring occasionally; then reduce heat and simmer for 10 minutes. Stir in port. Season to taste with salt and pepper Garnish each serving with sour cream, if desired.

makes 8 servings

per serving: 144 calories, 5 g protein, 21 g carbohydrates, 4 g total fat, 0 mg cholesterol, 73 mg sodium

chicken & capellini soup

preparation time: 25 minutes

1½ **pounds lemon-herb marinated boneless, skinless chicken breasts**

¾ **cup peeled baby-cut carrots**

2 **tablespoons butter or margarine**

2 **cans (about 14½ oz. *each*) fat-free reduced-sodium chicken broth**

½ **cup dry white wine**

2 **ounces dried capellini (angel hair pasta), broken in half**

8 **Swiss chard leaves**

2 **medium-size tomatoes**

⅓ **cup grated Parmesan cheese**

1 Cut chicken into bite-size pieces; set aside. Cut carrots in half lengthwise; set aside.

2 Melt butter in a 4- to 5-quart pan over medium-high heat. Add chicken and cook, stirring often, until no longer pink in center; cut to test (3 to 4 minutes).

3 Add carrots, broth, and wine. Bring to a boil over high heat; stir in capellini. Reduce heat and boil gently, uncovered, until carrots are tender to bite (6 to 7 minutes). Meanwhile, trim and discard tough stem bases from chard leaves; then cut chard stems and leaves into shreds. Seed and chop tomatoes.

4 Add chard and tomatoes to pan; cover and remove from heat. Let stand just until tomatoes are heated through (2 to 3 minutes). Sprinkle with cheese.

makes 5 servings (about 10 cups)

per serving: 312 calories, 31 g protein, 20 g carbohydrates, 10 g total fat, 89 mg cholesterol, 1,579 mg sodium

potato, cauliflower & watercress soup

preparation time: about 1 hour

1½ **cups cauliflower flowerets, cut into bite-size pieces**

2½ **cups nonfat milk**

2 **tablespoons margarine**

½ **cup slivered shallots**

⅛ **teaspoon ground nutmeg**

2 **large russet potatoes, peeled and diced**

1¾ **cups low-sodium chicken broth**

8 **cups lightly packed watercress sprigs**

Salt and freshly ground white pepper

¼ **to ⅓ cup plain lowfat yogurt or light sour cream**

1 In a 2- to 3-quart pan, combine cauliflower and milk. Bring to a boil over medium heat; reduce heat to medium-low and cook until cauliflower is tender when pierced (8 to 10 minutes). Place a strainer over a large bowl and pour cauliflower mixture through it; set cauliflower and milk aside separately.

2 Rinse pan; set over medium heat and add margarine. When margarine is melted, add shallots and nutmeg; cook, stirring occasionally, until shallots are soft but not browned (3 to 5 minutes). Add potatoes and broth; increase heat to medium-high and bring to a boil. Reduce heat, cover, and simmer until potatoes are very tender when pierced (about 15 to 20 minutes). Reserve several watercress sprigs for garnish, then stir remaining watercress into potato mixture and cook, uncovered, for 5 minutes. Add cauliflower to pan and cook until heated through (about 3 minutes).

3 In a blender or food processor, whirl potato mixture, half at a time, until smooth. Return to pan, add reserved milk, and heat just until steaming (do not boil). Season to taste with salt and white pepper: Garnish each serving with a dollop of yogurt and a watercress sprig.

makes 4 to 6 servings

per serving: 195 calories, 10 g protein, 27 g carbohydrates, 6 g total fat, 16 mg cholesterol, 179 mg sodium

newport red pepper chowder

preparation time: 45 to 50 minutes

¼ cup butter or margarine; or ¼ cup salad oil

2 medium-size onions, chopped

½ pound button mushrooms, sliced (optional)

1 tablespoon lemon juice

2 large red bell peppers, stemmed, seeded, and cut into thin strips

4 cups homemade chicken broth or 2 cans (14½ oz. *each*) regular-strength chicken broth

1 pound thin-skinned potatoes, scrubbed and sliced

2 tablespoons *each* cornstarch and water, stirred together

1 cup sour cream

1½ to 2 pounds boned, skinned white fish, such as halibut, rockfish, or sole

¼ cup minced parsley

Salt and pepper

Lemon wedges

Almost any white fleshed fish can be used in this red and white chowder; choose the type that's most economical when you shop.

1 Melt butter in a 4- to 5-quart pan over medium-high heat. Add onions, mushrooms (if used), lemon juice, and bell peppers; cook, stirring, until vegetables are barely soft, about 10 minutes. Add broth and potatoes. Bring to a boil over high heat; then reduce heat, cover, and simmer until potatoes are tender when pierced, about 15 minutes.

2 Stir together cornstarch-water mixture and sour cream. Gradually stir in some of the soup liquid; then, stirring constantly, pour back into pan and bring to a boil over high heat.

3 Meanwhile, rinse fish, pat dry, and cut into bite-size chunks. Add fish and parsley to soup. Return to a boil; reduce heat, cover, and simmer until fish flakes readily when prodded with a fork, about 2 minutes. If made ahead, let cool, then cover and refrigerate until next day. Reheat until steaming before serving. To serve, season soup to taste with salt and pepper; offer lemon wedges to squeeze into soup.

makes 6 to 8 servings

per serving: 318 calories, 25 g protein, 23 g carbohydrates, 14 g total fat, 78 mg cholesterol, 140 mg sodium

tortilla soup

preparation time: about 20 minutes

1 pound boned, skinned chicken breasts

2 fresh poblano chiles (also called pasillas)

½ cup chopped onion

8 cups fat-skimmed chicken broth

6 corn tortillas

About ¼ cup lime juice

1 Rinse chicken; cut into l-inch chunks.

2 Rinse chiles, then trim and discard stems, seeds, and veins. Cut chiles lengthwise into ⅛- to ¼-inch strips.

3 In a 4- to 5-quart pan over high heat, bring chiles, onion, and broth to a boil. Reduce heat, cover, and simmer 5 minutes. Add chicken, cover, and simmer until meat is no longer pink in center of thickest part (cut to test), about 4 minutes.

4 Meanwhile, cut tortillas into 1-inch squares. Divide squares equally among wide soup bowls.

5 Ladle soup over tortillas. Add lime juice to taste.

makes 4 servings

per serving: 299 calories, 45 g protein, 23 g carbohydrates, 2.4 g total fat, 66 mg cholesterol, 289 mg sodium

caldo xochilt

preparation time: 35 to 40 minutes

1 dried ancho (poblano), California (Anaheim), or New Mexico chile, stemmed and seeded

6 cups homemade chicken broth or 1 large can (49½ oz.) regular-strength chicken broth

2 tablespoons long-grain white rice

⅓ cup drained canned garbanzo beans

1 medium-size onion, chopped

2 tablespoons canned diced green chiles

1 medium-size firm-ripe tomato, peeled, cored, and chopped

1 medium-size firm-ripe avocado

2 limes, cut into wedges

½ cup chopped fresh cilantro

Salt

This Chile-seasoned soup (pronounced call-doh-soh-chilt) hails from Guadalajara. Add your choice of a simple tomato salsa, chopped onion, and avocado; then add a squeeze of lime.

1 Cover dried chile with boiling water and let stand for 10 minutes. Drain chile, then cut into large pieces.

2 In a 2- to 3-quart pan, bring broth to a boil; add chile pieces, rice, and garbanzos. Reduce heat, cover, and simmer until rice is tender to bite, about 15 minutes.

3 Meanwhile, in a small bowl, combine ¼ cup of the chopped onion with green chiles and tomato; set aside. Place remaining onion in another bowl. Pit, peel, and dice avocado; place in a third bowl. Squeeze some lime juice over avocado to prevent darkening.

4 Remove soup from heat and stir in cilantro. Season to taste with salt. Offer tomato mixture, chopped onion, avocado, and lime wedges to add to individual servings

makes 4 or 5 servings

per serving: 171 calories, 3 g protein, 22 g carbohydrates, 9 g total fat, 0 mg cholesterol, 80 mg sodium

shrimp & cannellini soup

preparation time: about 45 minutes

1 tablespoon salad oil

2 large onions, chopped

1 cup thinly sliced celery

3 cloves garlic, minced or pressed

2 cans (about 15 oz. *each*) cannellini beans, drained and rinsed

4 cups low-sodium chicken broth

¼ cup catsup

2 tablespoons dry sherry (optional)

⅓ pound small cooked shrimp

¼ cup chopped parsley

Salt and pepper

1 Heat oil in a 4- to 5-quart pan over medium-high heat. Add onions, celery, and garlic; cook, stirring often, until all vegetables are browned (about 20 minutes).

2 Transfer vegetable mixture to a food processor or blender; add half the beans and 2 cups of the broth. Whirl until smoothly puréed, then return to pan. Purée remaining beans with remaining 2 cups broth; add to pan. Stir in catsup and, if desired, sherry. (At this point, you may cover and refrigerate until next day.)

3 To serve, stir soup over medium heat until hot. Ladle soup into 4 bowls; top equally with shrimp and parsley. Season to taste with salt and pepper.

makes 4 servings

per serving: 303 calories, 23 g protein, 38 g carbohydrates, 7 g total fat, 73 mg cholesterol, 610 mg sodium

carrot & cilantro soup

preparation time: about 35 minutes

1½ pounds carrots

4 cups regular-strength chicken broth

¾ teaspoon curry powder

2 tablespoons lemon juice

Ground red pepper (cayenne)

¼ cup lightly packed chopped fresh cilantro

1 Cut carrots into ½-inch-thick slices and place in a 3- to 4-quart pan. Add broth and curry powder and bring to a boil over high heat; reduce heat, cover, and simmer until carrots are very soft (about 20 minutes). Stir in lemon juice.

2 In a blender or food processor, whirl soup, a portion at a time, until puréed. Season to taste with red pepper. Ladle soup into bowls and sprinkle cilantro over each portion.

makes 4 servings

per serving: 96 calories, 5 g protein, 17 g carbohydrates, 2 g total fat, 0 mg cholesterol, 1,042 mg sodium

lentil cream soup

preparation time: 10 to 15 minutes
cooking time: 30 minutes to 1½ hours, depending on type of lentil

½ cup lentils

4 cups homemade chicken broth or 2 cans (14½ oz. *each*) regular-strength chicken or beef broth

1 medium-size carrot, peeled

8 to 10 parsley sprigs

¼ teaspoon whole cloves

1 tablespoon olive oil or salad oil

½ cup chopped shallots or red onion

1 cup dry sherry

2 tablespoons lemon juice

2 cups whipping cream

½ teaspoon pepper

Edible flowers such as pansies or rose petals, rinsed (optional)

Whole chives (optional)

1 Sort lentils and remove any debris. Rinse lentils, drain, and place in a 2- to 3-quart pan; add broth, carrot, parsley sprigs, and cloves. Bring to a boil; reduce heat, cover, and simmer until lentils are very tender to bite-about 15 minutes for decorticated lentils, up to 1 hour for unskinned lentils. Discard carrot, parsley, and as many cloves as you can find.

2 Heat oil in a 5- to 6-quart pan over medium heat. Add shallots; cook until soft, stirring occasionally. Add sherry and lemon juice and boil over high heat, uncovered, until reduced to about ¼ cup. Stir in lentils and their cooking liquid, cream, and pepper. Heat to simmering, then pour into a tureen or bowls. Garnish with flowers and chives, if desired.

makes 6 to 8 servings

per serving: 277 calories, 5 g protein, 18 g carbohydrates, 21 g total fat, 66 mg cholesterol, 33 mg sodium

mediterranean minestrone

preparation time: 30 minutes

4 ounces mild Italian sausage

1 medium-size onion, coarsely chopped

2 cloves garlic, minced or pressed

1½ teaspoons dried thyme

¼ teaspoon pepper

1 large can (about 49½ oz.) fat-free reduced-sodium chicken broth

¾ cup water

2 large carrots, coarsely chopped

2 stalks celery, coarsely chopped

1 teaspoon grated lemon peel

1 package (about 9 oz.) frozen potato gnocchi

2 cups broccoli flowerets

1 medium-size tomato, cut into ¼-inch cubes

¼ cup grated Parmesan cheese

Croutons

1. Remove casings from sausage and crumble meat into a 5- to 6-quart pan. Add onion, garlic, thyme, and pepper. Cook over medium-high heat, stirring occasionally, until sausage is browned (4 to 5 minutes).

2. Add broth, water, carrots, celery, and lemon peel. Bring to a boil over high heat.

3. Add gnocchi and broccoli. Cook, uncovered, until gnocchi and vegetables are tender to bite (about 8 minutes). Top with tomato and sprinkle with cheese. Sprinkle with croutons, if desired.

makes 6 servings (about 12 cups)

per serving: 218 calories, 12 g protein, 26 g carbohydrates, 8 g total fat, 18 mg cholesterol, 917 mg sodium

cold avocado soup

preparation time: about 7 minutes

1 large ripe avocado

½ cup chilled half-and-half or whipping cream

1½ cups chilled regular-strength chicken broth

1 tablespoon lemon juice

Salt

Snipped chives or watercress sprigs (optional)

1. Pit and peel avocado; cut into chunks. In a blender, whirl avocado, half-and-half, broth, and lemon juice until smooth. (To prepare in a food processor, whirl avocado with half-and-half until puréed; add broth and lemon juice and whirl until smooth.) Season to taste with salt.

2. Ladle soup into wide, shallow bowls. Garnish each portion with chives, if desired.

makes 4 servings

per serving: 151 calories, 3 g protein, 7 g carbohydrates, 14 g total fat, 11 mg cholesterol, 389 mg sodium

beggar's bundle soup

preparation time: about 45 minutes

¼ **pound fresh shiitake mushrooms**

¼ **pound sliced cooked ham**

About 7 green onions (including tops)

½ **cup (½ of an 8-oz. can) sliced water chestnuts, drained and chopped**

3 cups chopped napa cabbage

1 tablespoon minced fresh ginger

2 cups fat-skimmed chicken broth

4 egg roll wrappers (6 in. square)

⅓ **cup fresh cilantro leaves**

1 Trim off and discard mushroom stems. Rinse caps, drain, and cut into ¼-inch slices. Cut ham into thin slivers. Trim off and discard root ends of green onions. Cut off 4 of the longest green spears from onion tops and set aside. Chop white parts of onions and enough of the remaining tops to make 1 cup. Discard remaining tops.

2 In a 5- to 6-quart nonstick pan over high heat, combine mushrooms, ham, ½ cup chopped onions, water chestnuts, cabbage, and ginger. Stir often until mixture is lightly browned, about 8 minutes. Spoon into a bowl.

3 Pour 1 cup water and enough of the broth into pan to make liquid 1 inch deep. Bring to a boil over high heat. Immerse reserved green onion tops in liquid just until wilted, ½ to 1 minute. Turn heat to low and set a rack in pan above liquid. Spoon ¼ of the mushroom mixture onto the center of each egg roll wrapper. Bring corners of wrapper together and tie with a green onion top to enclose filling.

4 Gently set bundles side by side on rack. Cover pan, turn heat to high, and steam until bundles are slightly translucent and egg roll wrappers are firm (cut a small piece from top to test), about 5 minutes. With 2 large spoons, gently transfer 1 or 2 bundles to each of 2 soup bowls. Add remaining broth and green onions to pan, bring to a boil, then ladle into bowls. Sprinkle bundles with cilantro leaves.

makes 2 servings

per serving: 253 calories, 26 g protein, 25 g carbohydrates, 5.7 g total fat, 1,043 mg sodium, 35 mg cholesterol

salsa fish soup

preparation time: about 25 minutes

6 cups fat-free reduced-sodium chicken broth

⅔ **cup regular or quick-cooking rice**

2 cups frozen corn kernels

1 pound skinned, boned mild flavored white-fleshed fish (such as rockfish or Lingcod), cut into 1-inch chunks

1 cup refrigerated or canned tomato-based chunk-style salsa; or 1 cup canned Mexican-style stewed tomatoes

Lime wedges

1 In a 5- to 6-quart pan, combine broth and rice. Bring to a boil over high heat. Reduce heat, cover, and simmer until rice is tender to bite (about 15 minutes; about 5 minutes for quick-cooking rice).

2 Add corn, fish, and salsa to pan. Cover and simmer soup until fish is just opaque in thickest part; cut to test (about 5 minutes). Offer lime wedges to squeeze into soup to taste.

makes 4 servings

per serving: 338 calories, 31 g protein, 48 g carbohydrates, 3 g total fat, 40 mg cholesterol, 1,679 mg sodium

ham & black bean soup

preparation time: 25 minutes

1 tablespoon vegetable oil

1 pound baked ham, cut into bite-size pieces

1 large onion, cut into thin slivers

1 large green bell pepper, seeded and chopped

2 cans (about 15 oz. *each*) black beans

2 cans (about 14½ oz. *each*) beef broth

⅔ cup water

¼ cup cider vinegar

2 large carrots, shredded

⅓ cup firmly packed light brown sugar

1 tablespoon dry mustard

1 teaspoon grated lemon peel

½ teaspoon liquid hot pepper seasoning

⅓ cup coarsely chopped parsley

1 Heat oil in a 5- to 6-quart pan over medium-high heat. Add ham, onion, and bell pepper; cook, stirring often, until vegetables are tender to bite (4 to 5 minutes).

2 Meanwhile, pour one can of the beans and their liquid into a food processor or blender; whirl until puréed. Pour purée into pan; stir in broth, water, and vinegar. Reserve ¼ cup of the carrots for garnish, if desired; to pan, add remaining carrots, sugar, mustard, lemon peel, and hot pepper seasoning. Bring to a boil; then reduce heat and simmer, uncovered, until flavors are blended (4 to 5 minutes).

3 Reduce heat to medium-low and add remaining can of beans and their liquid. Cook, stirring occasionally, until soup is bubbly and heated through (5 to 7 minutes). Sprinkle with parsley and, if desired, reserved carrots.

makes 6 servings (about 12 cups)

per serving: 367 calories, 27 g protein, 41 g carbohydrates, 11 g total fat, 45 mg cholesterol, 2,082 mg sodium

maritata soup

preparation time: about 25 minutes

12 cups beef broth

8 ounces dried vermicelli, broken into short lengths

½ cup freshly grated Parmesan cheese

⅓ cup Neufchâtel or nonfat cream cheese

3 large egg whites

If you're sodium sensitive, then you might want to use reduced-sodium beef broth in this recipe and slightly reduce the amount of Parmesan cheese.

1 Bring broth to a boil in a 5- to 6-quart pan over high heat. Stir in pasta; reduce heat, cover, and simmer just until pasta is tender to bite (8 to 10 minutes).

2 Meanwhile, beat Parmesan cheese, Neufchâtel cheese, and egg whites with an electric mixer or in a blender until well combined.

3 Slowly pour about 1 cup of the simmering broth into cheese mixture, mixing to combine. Then return cheese-broth mixture to pan, stirring constantly until hot (2 to 3 minutes).

makes 8 servings

per serving: 188 calories, 9 g protein, 22 g carbohydrates, 5 g total fat, 11 mg cholesterol, 2,613 mg sodium

salads

antipasto salad

preparation time: 30 minutes

¼ **cup red wine vinegar**

2 **tablespoons olive oil**

2 **tablespoons drained capers**

1 **tablespoon lemon juice**

¼ **teaspoon black pepper**

8 **to 12 ounces thinly sliced cold meats, such as salami, mortadella, and roast beef (choose 2 or 3 kinds)**

12 **cups mixed salad greens, rinsed and crisped**

1 **large yellow bell pepper seeded and cut into short, wide strips**

½ **cup firmly packed fresh basil leaves, chopped**

1 **jar (7 to 12 oz.) roasted red peppers, drained and patted dry**

2 **ounces Parmesan cheese, cut into thin shavings; or 2 ounces provolone cheese, cut into thin strips**

1 **can (about 2 oz.) anchovies, drained well (optional)**

Basil sprigs

1 In a small bowl, whisk vinegar, oil, capers, lemon juice, and black pepper to blend; set aside.

2 Cut sliced meats into short strips about ¼ inch wide (or cut each slice in half).

3 In a shallow serving bowl, mix greens, bell pepper, and chopped basil. Drizzle three-fourths of the dressing over greens; mix well. Decoratively arrange meats, roasted peppers, cheese, and anchovies (if desired) over greens. Drizzle with remaining dressing. Garnish with basil sprigs.

makes 4 servings

per serving: 488 calories, 24 g protein, 17 g carbohydrates, 35 g total fat, 66 mg cholesterol, 1,916 mg sodium

bouquet salad mix

preparation time: about 10 minutes

¼ **cup orange juice**

1 **tablespoon lemon juice**

1 **tablespoon extra-virgin olive oil**

½ **teaspoon grated orange peel**

2 **quarts salad mix, rinsed and drained**

3 **cups edible blossoms or petals rinsed and drained**

Salt and pepper

In a wide bowl, combine orange juice, lemon juice, oil, and orange peel. Add salad mix and blossoms. Mix and season to taste with salt and pepper.

makes 6 servings

per serving: 36 calories, 0.6 g protein, 3.1 g carbohydrates, 2.3 g total fat, 0 mg cholesterol, 7.7 mg sodium

stir-fried pork & escarole salad

preparation time: about 30 minutes

3 quarts lightly packed rinsed, crisped escarole or spinach leaves

²/₃ cup cider vinegar

3 tablespoons honey

2 large Red Delicious apples, cored and thinly sliced

4 teaspoons cornstarch

1 cup fat-free reduced-sodium chicken broth

2 teaspoons Dijon mustard

½ teaspoon dried thyme

2 teaspoons olive oil

2 large shallots, chopped

1 pound lean boneless pork loin, loin end, or leg, trimmed of fat and cut into paper-thin ½- by 3-inch slices

1 cup raisins

1 Place escarole on a wide serving platter. In a medium-size bowl, stir together vinegar, honey, and apples. Then remove apples with a slotted spoon and scatter over escarole. Add cornstarch, broth, mustard, and thyme to vinegar mixture in bowl; stir well and set aside.

2 Heat oil in a wide nonstick frying pan or wok over medium-high heat. When oil is hot, add shallots and pork and stir-fry until meat is lightly browned (about 3 minutes). Push meat to one side of pan. Stir vinegar mixture well, pour into pan, and stir just until boiling (about 1 minute). Stir meat into sauce; then quickly spoon meat mixture over escarole and sprinkle with raisins.

makes 4 servings

per serving: 443 calories, 28 g protein, 67 g carbohydrates, 9 g total fat, 67 mg cholesterol, 305 mg sodium

wilted spinach salad with oranges

preparation time: about 25 minutes

2 medium-size oranges

2 quarts lightly packed spinach leaves, rinsed and crisped

1 large onion, thinly sliced and separated into rings

¼ cup balsamic or red wine vinegar

2 teaspoons vegetable oil

1 teaspoon dried tarragon

1 Grate 1 teaspoon peel (colored part only) from one of the oranges; set aside. With a sharp knife, cut remaining peel and all white membrane from both oranges. Holding fruit over a bowl to catch juice, cut between membranes to free segments; place segments in bowl with juice and set aside. Place spinach in a large salad bowl.

2 In a wide frying pan, combine onion, vinegar, oil, tarragon, and grated orange peel. Place over medium-low heat, cover, and cook until onions are tender-crisp when pierced (6 to 8 minutes). Gently stir in orange segments and juice. Pour orange mixture over spinach. Mix lightly, then serve at once.

makes 4 servings

per serving: 103 calories, 4 g protein, 18 g carbohydrates, 3 g total fat, 0 mg cholesterol, 70 mg sodium

watercress, butter lettuce & shrimp salad

preparation time: about 35 minutes

1 tablespoon mustard seeds

¼ cup boiling water

Olive oil cooking spray

2 ½ cups ½-inch cubes sourdough French bread

¼ cup balsamic or red wine vinegar

2 teaspoons Dijon mustard

1 tablespoon olive oil

2 ½ quarts torn butter lettuce leaves, rinsed and crisped

2 ½ quarts lightly packed watercress sprigs, rinsed and crisped

8 ounces small cooked shrimp

1 Place mustard seeds in a small bowl; pour boiling water over them. Let stand for at least 10 minutes or up to 8 hours; drain well.

2 Spray a shallow rimmed baking pan with cooking spray. Spread bread cubes in pan; spray with cooking spray. Bake in a 350° oven until crisp and golden brown (12 to 15 minutes). Let cool in pan on a rack. (At this point, you may store airtight at room temperature for up to 2 days.)

3 In a small bowl, stir together mustard seeds, vinegar, mustard, and oil. Arrange lettuce, watercress, and shrimp in a large salad bowl; add mustard seed dressing and mix lightly until greens are coated. Top salad with croutons.

makes 6 servings

per serving: 123 calories, 12 g protein, 10 g carbohydrates, 4 g total fat, 74 mg cholesterol, 229 mg sodium

litchi, penne & chicken salad

preparation time: about 40 minutes

5 ounces dried penne

1 can (about 11 oz.) litchis

¾ cup plain low-fat yogurt

¾ teaspoon grated lemon peel

4 teaspoons lemon juice

1½ teaspoons dried thyme

2 cups bite-size pieces cooked chicken

½ cup finely diced celery

8 large butter lettuce leaves, rinsed and crisped

⅓ cup chopped green onions

Salt and pepper

1 Bring 8 cups water to a boil in a 4- to 5-quart pan over medium-high heat. Stir in pasta and cook just until tender to bite (8 to 10 minutes); or cook according to package directions. Drain, rinse with cold water until cool, and drain well.

2 Drain litchis, reserving ⅓ cup of the syrup; set fruit aside. In a large nonmetal bowl, mix reserved ⅓ cup litchi syrup, yogurt, lemon peel, lemon juice, and thyme. Add pasta, chicken, and celery. Mix thoroughly but gently. (At this point, you may cover pasta mixture and fruit separately and refrigerate for up to 4 hours; stir pasta occasionally.)

3 Arrange lettuce on individual plates. Top with pasta mixture and litchis. Sprinkle with onions. Offer salt and pepper to add to taste.

makes 4 servings

per serving: 358 calories, 28 g protein, 47 g carbohydrates, 7 g total fat, 65 mg cholesterol, 136 mg sodium

turkey & white bean salad

preparation time: about 30 minutes

2 turkey breast tenderloins (about 1 lb. *total*)

½ cup cider vinegar

¼ cup fat-free reduced-sodium chicken broth

2 tablespoons olive oil

1 teaspoon crumbled dried sage

1 teaspoon sugar

2 cans (about 15 oz. *each*) cannellini
   (white kidney beans), rinsed and drained

1 ¼ pounds firm-ripe pear-shaped (Roma-type)
   tomatoes

6 to 8 large red leaf lettuce leaves, rinsed
   and crisped

4 slices bacon, crisply cooked, drained,
   and crumbled

1 Rinse turkey and pat dry. In a 4- to 5-quart pan, bring about 2 quarts water to a boil over high heat. Add turkey, cover, and immediately remove pan from heat; let stand, undisturbed, until you are ready to check for doneness (about 20 minutes). To check, quickly cut a small slit in center of thickest part of turkey; if meat is no longer pink, remove from water. If it is still pink, immediately return to hot water, cover, and let stand until no longer pink, checking every 5 minutes. Immerse turkey in ice water until cool, then drain and pat dry. Cut turkey diagonally into ½-inch-thick slices.

2 While turkey is steeping, combine vinegar, broth, oil, sage, and sugar in a small bowl; whisk to blend. In a large bowl, combine beans and a third of the dressing; mix gently. Thinly slice tomatoes and set aside.

3 To serve, arrange lettuce leaves on a platter. Spoon bean salad over lettuce. Decoratively arrange turkey and tomatoes alongside beans. Drizzle with remaining dressing and sprinkle with bacon.

makes 4 servings

per serving: 427 calories, 40 g protein, 39 g carbohydrates, 12 g total fat, 76 mg cholesterol, 648 mg sodium

sweet potato & apple salad with ginger dressing

preparation time: 30 minutes

6 small sweet potatoes or yams, scrubbed (choose
   slimmer sweet potatoes for faster cooking)

2 tablespoons honey

1 teaspoon grated lemon peel

1 tablespoon lemon juice

¾ teaspoon ground ginger (or to taste)

½ teaspoon ground cinnamon

1 cup plain nonfat yogurt

2 large red-skinned apples

¾ cup thinly sliced celery

½ cup salted roasted peanuts or almonds

Salt

1 Place potatoes in a 5- to 6-quart pan and add enough water to cover. Bring to a boil; then reduce heat, cover, and simmer just until barely tender when pierced (20 to 25 minutes). Drain. Immerse potatoes in ice water until cool, then drain and pat dry.

2 Meanwhile, in a large bowl, whisk honey, lemon peel, lemon juice, ginger, cinnamon, and yogurt to blend. Core apples and cut into ¾-inch cubes. Add apples, celery, and three-fourths of the peanuts to dressing; mix well.

3 Peel potatoes and cut into ¾-inch cubes; mix gently with apple mixture. Season to taste with salt. Sprinkle with remaining peanuts.

makes 8 servings

per serving: 204 calories, 6 g protein, 37 g carbohydrates, 5 g total fat, 1 mg cholesterol, 82 mg sodium

warm turkey & bacon salad

preparation time: about 20 minutes

¼ **cup olive oil**

3 **tablespoons mayonnaise**

3 **tablespoons white wine vinegar**

1 **tablespoon Dijon mustard**

1 **teaspoon dried thyme**

12 **cups bite-size pieces butter lettuce, rinsed and crisped**

1 **large firm-ripe tomato, cut into wedges**

1 **large red or yellow bell pepper, seeded and cut into thin, short strips**

¼ **cup thinly sliced green onions**

4 **slices bacon, cut into thin slivers**

1 **pound boneless, skinless turkey thigh, cut into thin strips**

About ¼ **cup grated Parmesan cheese**

Belgian endive spears, rinsed and crisped (optional)

1 In a small bowl, whisk oil, mayonnaise, vinegar, mustard, and thyme to blend smoothly; set aside.

2 In a large bowl, arrange lettuce, tomato, bell pepper, and onions.

3 In a wide frying pan, cook bacon over medium-high heat, stirring occasionally, until crisp (4 to 5 minutes). With a slotted spoon, lift out bacon, drain, and set aside. Discard all but 1 tablespoon of the drippings from pan.

4 Increase heat to high. Add turkey and cook, stirring often, until lightly browned (3 to 4 minutes). Immediately pour turkey and pan juices over lettuce mixture; then add bacon, dressing, and ¼ cup of the cheese. Mix well. Sprinkle with additional cheese and garnish with endive spears, if desired. Serve at once.

makes 4 servings

per serving: 456 calories, 29 g protein, 9 g carbohydrates, 34 g total fat, 103 mg cholesterol, 460 mg sodium

melon, basil & prosciutto salad

preparation time: 15 minutes

12 **to 16 large butter lettuce leaves, rinsed and crisped**

4 **slices prosciutto**

1 **tablespoon firmly packed brown sugar**

8 **cups bite-size cubes of peeled, seeded honeydew melon**

¼ **cup finely slivered fresh basil**

About 2 tablespoons balsamic vinegar

2 **ounces Parmesan cheese, cut into thin shavings**

Pepper

Basil sprigs

1 Arrange lettuce leaves, overlapping if necessary, on a rimmed platter.

2 Cut prosciutto into strips about 1 inch long and ¼ inch wide. Place in a large bowl, add sugar, and toss lightly to coat.

3 Add melon and slivered basil; mix well. Spoon melon mixture over lettuce leaves and drizzle with vinegar. Top with cheese and sprinkle with pepper. Garnish with basil sprigs. Serve immediately (the basil's flavor grows stronger upon standing and can overpower the delicate melon).

makes 4 servings

per serving: 243 calories, 13 g protein, 36 g carbohydrates, 7 g total fat, 27 mg cholesterol, 658 mg sodium

chinese chicken salad

preparation time: about 30 minutes

4 to 5 ounces cellophane noodles (saifun; made from bean or yam, not rice)

1 package (about 6 oz.) frozen Chinese pea pods, thawed

½ cup seasoned rice vinegar

3 tablespoons soy sauce

4 teaspoons minced fresh ginger

1 tablespoon sugar

1 tablespoon dry mustard blended with 1 tablespoon cold water

1 tablespoon Asian sesame oil

6 cups mixed salad greens, rinsed and crisped

½ cup finely chopped cilantro

1 tablespoon vegetable oil

2 large red or yellow bell peppers, seeded and chopped

1 cup thinly sliced red onion

2 tablespoons lemon juice

2 cloves garlic, thinly sliced

3 cups shredded cooked chicken breast

1 In a 4- to 5-quart pan, bring about 2 quarts water to a boil over high heat. Stir in noodles; reduce heat and boil gently for 5 minutes. Remove pan from heat and let stand until noodles are tender to bite (5 to 10 minutes). Transfer to a strainer to drain. Leaving noodles in strainer, snip them with scissors into smaller strands; then stir in pea pods. Set aside to drain.

2 In a small bowl, whisk vinegar, soy sauce, ginger, sugar, mustard mixture, and sesame oil to blend. Set aside.

3 In a large bowl, combine greens and two-thirds of the cilantro. Transfer to a large platter.

4 Heat vegetable oil in a wide frying pan over medium-high heat. Add bell peppers, onion, lemon juice, and garlic. Cook, stirring often, until onion is soft (about 5 minutes); add water, 1 tablespoon at a time, if pan appears dry. With a slotted spoon, transfer onion mixture to bowl used to mix greens. Mix in chicken.

5 Shake noodles and pea pods in strainer to remove any remaining water; then return to noodle cooking pan and mix with a third of the dressing. Mound noodle mixture on greens; top with chicken mixture. Drizzle with remaining dressing. Sprinkle with remaining cilantro.

makes 6 servings

per serving: 315 calories, 25 g protein, 36 g carbohydrates, 8 g total fat, 60 mg cholesterol, 977 mg sodium

green bean & jicama salad

preparation time: about 30 minutes

5 tablespoons white wine vinegar

⅔ cup thinly slivered red onion

¾ pound green beans, ends removed

1 pound jicama, peeled

⅓ cup olive oil or salad oil

2 teaspoons Dijon mustard

Salt and pepper

1 In a small bowl, combine 1½ cups cold water with 2 tablespoons of the vinegar. Add onion and let stand for 20 minutes.

2 Meanwhile, pull beans through a French bean cutter or slice into thin strips with a knife. Place beans on a rack above ½ inch boiling water in a 5- to 6-quart pan; cover and steam until tender (3 to 4 minutes). Plunge beans into ice water and stir until cool; then drain. Cut jicama into matchstick-size pieces.

3 In a large salad bowl, whisk together oil, mustard, and remaining 3 tablespoons vinegar. Drain onion and add to dressing along with beans and jicama; mix to coat well. Season to taste with salt and pepper.

makes 6 to 8 servings

per serving: 136 calories, 2 g protein, 10 g carbohydrates, 10 g total fat, 0 mg cholesterol, 49 mg sodium

black bean & jicama salad

preparation time: about 15 minutes

1 can (about 15 oz.) black beans, drained
    and rinsed; or 2 cups cooked black beans,
    drained and rinsed

1 cup peeled, finely chopped jicama

¼ cup crumbled panela or feta cheese

3 tablespoons lime juice

⅓ cup minced cilantro

2 tablespoons thinly sliced green onion

2 teaspoons honey

¼ teaspoon crushed red pepper flakes

4 to 8 butter leaves, rinsed and crisped

1 In a bowl, combine beans, jicama, cheese, lime juice, cilantro, onion, honey, and red pepper flakes. Mix well. (At this point, you may cover and refrigerate for up to 4 hours.)

2 To serve, spoon bean mixture into lettuce leaves.

makes 4 servings

per serving: 164 calories, 9 g protein, 28 g carbohydrates, 2 g total fat, 8 mg cholesterol, 100 mg sodium

mizuna, fennel & crab salad

preparation time: about 20 minutes

12 ounces fennel

⅔ pound mizuna, bare stems trimmed,
    leaves rinsed and crisped

⅔ cup plain nonfat yogurt

¼ cup reduced-fat sour cream

2 tablespoons lemon juice

1 tablespoon Dijon mustard

1 teaspoon dried tarragon

½ teaspoon sugar

1½ pounds cooked crabmeat

1 Cut feathery tops from fennel; chop tops and set aside for dressing. Cut root ends and any bruised spots from fennel head; then thinly slice (you should have 2 cups) and place in a large bowl.

2 Reserve ¾ cup of the mizuna for dressing. Cut remaining mizuna into 2- to 3-inch long pieces; add to bowl with fennel.

3 To prepare dressing, in a blender or food processor, combine the ¾ cup reserved mizuna, yogurt, sour cream, lemon juice, mustard, 1 tablespoon of the reserved chopped fennel tops, tarragon, and sugar. Whirl until puréed; set aside.

4 Mound crab on mizuna mixture, placing the most attractive crab pieces on top. At the table, add dressing to salad; mix gently.

makes 6 servings

per serving: 172 calories, 27 g protein, 7 g carbohydrates, 4 g total fat, 117 mg cholesterol, 460 mg sodium

shrimp & spinach slaw

preparation time: about 25 minutes

4 cups finely shredded green cabbage

3 cups thinly sliced spinach leaves

1 medium-size cucumber, peeled and sliced

2 medium-size celery stalks, sliced

⅔ cup plain nonfat yogurt

3 tablespoons reduced-calorie mayonnaise

½ cup thinly sliced green onions

1 teaspoon grated lemon peel

2 tablespoons lemon juice

1 tablespoon sugar

About 12 large spinach leaves, rinsed and crisped (optional)

¾ to 1 pound small cooked shrimp

Lemon wedges

Salt and pepper

1 To prepare salad, in a large bowl, combine cabbage, sliced spinach leaves, cucumber, and celery.

2 To prepare yogurt-lemon dressing, in a small bowl, combine yogurt, mayonnaise, onions, lemon peel, lemon juice, and sugar. (At this point, you may cover and refrigerate the salad and dressing separately until next day.)

3 Add dressing to salad and mix well. If using large spinach leaves, use them to garnish salad in bowl; or arrange them around rim of a large platter and mound salad in center. Sprinkle shrimp over salad. Offer lemon wedges to squeeze over salad to taste; season to taste with salt and pepper.

makes 8 servings

per serving: 107 calories, 13 g protein, 9 g carbohydrates, 3 g total fat, 100 mg cholesterol, 189 mg sodium

mango, pear & avocado salad

preparation time: 20 minutes

½ cup balsamic vinegar

3 tablespoons honey

8 ounces packaged triple-washed spinach

2 large firm-ripe pears

2 tablespoons lemon juice

1 large avocado

2 large firm-ripe mangoes

3 ounces feta cheese, crumbled

Pepper

1 In a small bowl, whisk vinegar and honey to blend. In a large bowl, combine spinach and a fourth of the vinegar mixture; mix well. Arrange spinach on a platter or 4 to 6 individual plates.

2 Peel and core pears; cut into ½-inch-thick slices, combine with 1 tablespoon of the lemon juice, and set aside. Pit and peel avocado; cut into ½-inch-thick slices and combine with remaining 1 tablespoon lemon juice. Peel mangoes; cut fruit away from pits in ½-inch-thick slices.

3 Arrange pears, avocado, mangoes, and cheese over spinach. Offer pepper and remaining vinegar-honey mixture to add to taste.

makes 4 to 6 servings

per serving: 303 calories, 6 g protein, 56 g carbohydrates, 10 g total fat, 15 mg cholesterol, 235 mg sodium

indian-spiced garbanzo beans with cucumber & cabbage slaw

preparation time: about 20 minutes

6 cups shredded cabbage

1 medium-size cucumber, halved and thinly sliced

2 tablespoons lemon juice

1 tablespoon olive oil

2 tablespoons butter or margarine

1 large red bell pepper, seeded and cut into thin strips

1 large onion, halved and thinly sliced

1 tablespoon ground cumin

1 teaspoon ground coriander

½ teaspoon salt (or to taste)

⅛ teaspoon ground red pepper (cayenne)

2 cans (about 15 oz. *each*) garbanzo beans, rinsed and drained

½ cup chopped cilantro

½ cup sour cream

1 In a large bowl, combine cabbage, cucumber, lemon juice, and oil; mix well.

2 Melt butter in a wide nonstick frying pan over medium-high heat. Add bell pepper, onion, cumin, coriander, salt, and ground red pepper. Cook, stirring often, until onion is soft and beginning to brown (about 7 minutes). Add beans and ¼ cup water. Cook, stirring often, until beans are heated through (about 3 minutes); add water, 1 tablespoon at a time, if pan appears dry.

3 Remove pan from heat and stir in three-fourths of the cilantro. Spoon bean mixture over cabbage. Sprinkle with remaining cilantro. Offer sour cream to add to taste.

makes 4 servings

per serving: 353 calories, 11 g protein, 37 g carbohydrates, 19 g total fat, 28 mg cholesterol, 606 mg sodium

watermelon-mint salad

preparation time: about 15 minutes

1 watermelon (about 6 lbs.)

¾ cup slivered mild white onion

½ cup minced fresh mint

3 tablespoons cider vinegar

1 teaspoon chili powder

6 tablespoons salad oil

Salt

1 Slice watermelon into 1-inch-thick rounds; remove and discard rind. Cut flesh into 1-inch cubes; remove visible seeds. Place cubes in a large serving bowl, add onion and mint, and mix gently.

2 In a small bowl, whisk together vinegar, chili powder, and oil. Pour dressing over salad and mix to coat well. Season to taste with salt.

makes 8 servings

per serving: 155 calories, 1 g protein, 14 g carbohydrates, 11 g total fat, 0 mg cholesterol, 7 mg sodium

oriental salad

preparation time: about 40 minutes

6 cups lightly packed rinsed,
  crisped spinach leaves

¼ cup unseasoned rice vinegar
  or white wine vinegar

2 tablespoons reduced-sodium soy sauce

2 teaspoons honey

1 teaspoon Asian sesame oil

2 teaspoons sesame seeds

2 teaspoons vegetable oil

5 cups broccoli flowerets

1 pound carrots, cut into ¼-inch
  diagonal slices

1½ cups thinly sliced celery

1 medium-size onion, thinly sliced

1 Arrange spinach leaves on a large platter; cover and set aside. In a small bowl, stir together vinegar, soy sauce, honey, and sesame oil; set aside.

2 In a wide nonstick frying pan or wok, stir sesame seeds over medium heat until golden (about 3 minutes). Pour out of pan and set aside. Heat 1 teaspoon of the vegetable oil in pan over medium-high heat. When oil is hot, add half of the broccoli, carrots, celery, and onion. Stir-fry until vegetables are hot and bright in color (about 3 minutes). Add ⅓ cup water to pan, cover, and cook until vegetables are just tender to bite (about 3 minutes). Uncover and continue to cook, stirring, until liquid has evaporated (1 to 2 more minutes). Remove vegetables from pan and set aside. Repeat to cook remaining broccoli, carrots, celery, and onion, using remaining 1 teaspoon vegetable oil and adding ⅓ cup water after the first 3 minutes of cooking.

3 Return all cooked vegetables to pan and stir in vinegar mixture. Spoon vegetables onto spinach-lined platter and sprinkle with sesame seeds.

makes 6 servings

per serving: 118 calories, 6 g protein, 20 g carbohydrates, 3 g total fat, 0 mg cholesterol, 297 mg sodium

smoked trout & onion salad

preparation time: about 20 minutes

1 medium-size red onion, thinly sliced

¼ cup distilled white vinegar

¼ cup sour cream

1 tablespoon lemon juice

2 teaspoons prepared horseradish

1 tablespoon chopped fresh dill

1 large head romaine lettuce, separated into
  leaves, rinsed, and crisped

12 ounces smoked trout, boned, skinned, and
  cut or torn into ½-inch pieces

Dill sprigs (optional)

1 Place onion slices in a deep bowl and add enough cold water to cover. With your hands, squeeze slices until they are almost limp. Drain, rinse, and drain again.

2 Return onion to bowl and add vinegar and about 2 cups *each* ice cubes and water. Let stand until onion is crisp (about 15 minutes); drain well. Remove onion from bowl.

3 While onion is soaking, in a small bowl, whisk sour cream, lemon juice, horseradish, and chopped dill to blend smoothly; set aside.

4 Line each of 4 individual plates with 2 or 3 large lettuce leaves. Cut remaining lettuce crosswise into ¼-inch-wide strips.

5 In a large bowl, gently mix lettuce strips, trout, and onion. Add dressing and mix gently but thoroughly. Divide salad equally among lettuce-lined plates; garnish with dill sprigs, if desired. Serve immediately.

makes 4 servings

per serving: 240 calories, 24 g protein, 9 g carbohydrates, 12 g total fat, 29 mg cholesterol, 911 mg sodium

warm cioppino salad

preparation time: about 30 minutes

¼ cup lemon juice

1 teaspoon dried basil

1 teaspoon dried oregano

2 cloves garlic, minced or pressed

3 quarts lightly packed rinsed, crisped spinach
leaves, torn into bite-size pieces

1 tablespoon olive oil

8 ounces extra-large raw shrimp
(26 to 30 per lb.), shelled and deveined

2 cups thinly sliced mushrooms

2 cups thinly sliced zucchini

1 can (about 14½ oz.) tomatoes,
drained and chopped

12 pitted ripe olives

8 ounces cooked crabmeat

1 To prepare lemon dressing, in a small bowl, stir together lemon juice, basil, oregano, and garlic; set aside.

2 Place spinach in a wide serving bowl, cover, and set aside.

3 Heat oil in a wide nonstick frying pan or wok over medium-high heat. When oil is hot, add shrimp and stir-fry until just opaque in center; cut to test (3 to 4 minutes). Remove from pan with tongs or a slotted spoon and set aside.

4 Add mushrooms and zucchini to pan; stir-fry until zucchini is just tender to bite (about 3 minutes). Return shrimp to pan; add tomatoes, olives, and lemon dressing. Stir until mixture is heated through. Pour shrimp mixture over spinach, top with crab, and mix gently but thoroughly.

makes 6 servings

per serving: 149 calories, 18 g protein, 10 g carbohydrates, 5 g total fat, 85 mg cholesterol, 380 mg sodium

corn cobb salad

preparation time: about 20 minutes

⅓ cup olive oil

3 tablespoons red wine vinegar

1 tablespoon Dijon mustard

1 tablespoon minced shallot or red onion

1 cup crumbled feta cheese

2 medium-size ears corn

9 ounces packaged triple-washed spinach

½ cup salted roasted cashews

1 cup tiny bite-size cherry tomatoes

1 very small red onion, halved and thinly sliced

1 In a shallow bowl, whisk oil, vinegar, mustard, and shallot to blend. Stir in ¼ cup of the cheese; set aside.

2 Remove and discard husks and silk from corn. In a shallow bowl, hold one ear of corn upright, and, with a sharp knife, cut kernels from cob. Then, using blunt edge of knife, scrape juice from cob into another shallow bowl. Repeat with remaining ear of corn. Discard cobs. Stir corn juice into dressing.

3 To assemble salad, remove and discard any coarse stems from spinach. Then, in a wide serving bowl, combine spinach and half the dressing. Mound corn, remaining ¾ cup cheese, cashews, and tomatoes in separate sections atop spinach; place onion in center. Offer remaining dressing to add to taste.

makes 4 to 6 servings

per serving: 349 calories, 9 g protein, 21 g carbohydrates, 27 g total fat, 24 mg cholesterol, 497 mg sodium

japanese crab & radish salad

preparation time: about 15 minutes

1 small cucumber

1 green onion (including top), white and green part separated

10 medium-size radishes

½ to 1 pound cooked crabmeat

⅓ to ½ cup seasoned rice vinegar

1 teaspoon toasted black sesame seeds (optional)

1 Cut cucumber in half crosswise; then cut each half lengthwise into quarters. Set aside.

2 To prepare in a food processor, pack onion (white part only) and as many radishes as will fit into feed tube and slice; repeat to slice remaining radishes. Pack cucumber into feed tube and slice. Remove slicer and spread crabmeat over cucumber. Invert salad onto a large platter, spreading out slightly.

3 To prepare by hand, slice onion (white part only), radishes, and cucumber as thinly as possible. Spread crabmeat on platter and arrange vegetables in layers on top.

4 Pour vinegar over salad. Slice green portion of onion into long, thin strands and scatter over salad; sprinkle with sesame seeds, if desired.

makes 4 servings

per serving: 116 calories, 18 g protein, 7 g carbohydrates, 2 g total fat, 85 mg cholesterol, 242 mg sodium

shanghai tofu & peanut salad

preparation time: 40 to 45 minutes

1 package (about 1 lb.) medium-firm tofu

Salad oil

Sesame Dressing (recipe follows)

¾ pound bean sprouts

1 medium-size cucumber

⅔ cup shredded carrot

3 green onions (including tops), thinly sliced

¾ cup coarsely chopped salted peanuts

1 Cut tofu crosswise into 1-inch-thick slices. Place in a colander; rinse with cold water and let drain for 10 minutes, then place between paper towels and gently press out excess water. Place tofu on a wire rack in a shallow baking pan and brush all surfaces with oil.

2 Bake in a 350° oven for 20 minutes. Let cool, then cut into small, thin strips (about ¼ by ¼ by 1 inch). Prepare Sesame Dressing; add tofu, stirring gently to coat. Set aside.

3 Drop bean sprouts into a 5- to 6-quart pan half filled with boiling water. Cook until water returns to a full rolling boil; then drain, rinse with cold water, and drain again.

4 Peel cucumber, if desired, and cut in half lengthwise. Scoop out and discard seeds; cut cucumber into thin slices. Just before serving, add bean sprouts, cucumber, carrot, onions, and peanuts to tofu mixture; toss gently.

makes 4 to 6 servings

SESAME DRESSING

In a large salad bowl, stir together ¼ cup white wine vinegar, 2 table-spoons *each* sugar and salad oil, 1 tablespoon soy sauce, 1½ teaspoons Asian sesame oil, and ¼ teaspoon ground red pepper (cayenne).

per serving: 357 calories, 15 g protein, 19 g carbohydrates, 27 g total fat, 0 mg cholesterol, 413 mg sodium

spinach and radicchio salad with grapefruit

preparation time: about 45 minutes

¼ cup pine nuts

2 ruby or pink grapefruits

¼ cup olive oil

2 tablespoons balsamic vinegar

4 cups baby spinach leaves, rinsed and crisped

4 cups bite-size pieces radicchio leaves, rinsed and crisped

½ cup pitted prunes, cut into thin slivers

3 tablespoons thinly sliced green onions (including tops)

Salt and pepper

1 In a 6- to 8-inch frying pan over medium heat, stir or shake pine nuts until golden, about 5 minutes. Cool.

2 With a small, sharp knife, cut peel and white membrane from grapefruit. Over a bowl, cut between inner membranes and fruit, lifting out segments; reserve juice for another use.

3 In a wide bowl, whisk oil with vinegar. Add spinach, radicchio, prunes, and green onions; arrange grapefruit and nuts on salad. Mix; adding salt and pepper to taste.

makes about 6 servings

per serving: 171 calories, 3 g protein, 16 g carbohydrates, 12 g total fat, 0 mg cholesterol, 22 mg sodium

salad lyonnaise

preparation time: about 30 minutes

8 cups frisée or tender inner curly endive leaves, rinsed and crisped

About ¼ pound French bread, sliced and toasted

½ pound side bacon, cut into ¼-inch pieces

3 or 4 large eggs

¼ cup white wine vinegar

1 tablespoon Dijon mustard

Salt and pepper

1 Tear frisée into bite-size pieces and place in a wide salad bowl.

2 Tear bread into ½-inch chunks and scatter over the greens.

3 Put bacon in a 10- to 12-inch nonstick frying pan over medium heat and stir often until browned and crisp, 10 to 12 minutes. With a slotted spoon, transfer to towels to drain.

4 Break eggs into drippings in pan, and when whites are firm on the bottom, slide a spatula under each egg and, if desired, carefully turn over. Cook until whites are no longer clear, about 1 minute total. With spatula, transfer eggs to a plate (place side by side); keep warm.

5 Quickly discard all but 2 tablespoons fat from pan. Turn heat to high, add vinegar and mustard, and whisk until mixture boils.

6 Pour hot dressing over frisée and bread, add bacon, and mix. Spoon into wide bowls and top each serving with a hot egg. Season to taste with salt and pepper.

makes 3 or 4 servings

per serving: 483 calories, 14 g protein, 18 g carbohydrates, 39 g total fat, 251 mg cholesterol, 727 mg sodium

taco salad with chipotle cream

preparation time: about 20 minutes

¼ cup honey

¼ cup lime juice

2 to 3 teaspoons minced canned chipotle chiles in adobado sauce

1 tablespoon Dijon mustard

2 cloves garlic, minced or pressed

½ teaspoon ground cumin

¼ teaspoon ground allspice

¼ teaspoon salt

¼ cup sour cream

¼ cup chopped cilantro

12 cups shredded iceberg lettuce

¾ to 1 pound cooked roast beef or steak, shredded

½ cup shredded sharp Cheddar cheese

2 medium-size tomatoes, cut into wedges

1 large avocado, pitted, peeled, and sliced

1 cup corn chips or tortilla chips

1 In a small bowl, whisk honey, lime juice, chiles, mustard, garlic, cumin, allspice, and salt to blend smoothly. Whisk in sour cream until smooth. Stir in cilantro; set aside.

2 Divide lettuce equally among 4 wide, rimmed bowls. Top evenly with beef. Decoratively arrange cheese, tomatoes, avocado, and corn chips on each salad. Drizzle with dressing.

makes 4 servings

per serving: 516 calories, 29 g protein, 48 g carbohydrates, 26 g total fat, 65 mg cholesterol, 1,532 mg sodium

greens plus

preparation time: about 15 minutes

2 heads butter lettuce, separated into leaves, rinsed, and crisped

3 tablespoons pine nuts or slivered blanched almonds

2 large oranges

¼ cup unseasoned rice vinegar

1 tablespoon salad oil

½ teaspoon dry basil

1 Tear lettuce into bite-size pieces and place in a large salad bowl.

2 Toast nuts in a small frying pan over low heat until golden (3 to 5 minutes), shaking pan often. Let cool.

3 With a sharp knife, cut and peel all white membrane from oranges. Separate into segments. Add oranges and nuts to lettuce; toss to mix.

4 In a small bowl, whisk together vinegar, oil, and basil; pour over salad and toss well.

makes 4 servings

per serving: 124 calories, 3 g protein, 15 g carbohydrates, 7 g total fat, 0 mg cholesterol, 4 mg sodium

spinach & shrimp salad with tri-mustard dressing

preparation time: about 15 minutes

10 ounces packaged triple-washed baby spinach

1 pound shelled, deveined cooked shrimp (31 to 40 per lb.); leave tails on, if desired

6 tablespoons olive oil

¼ cup balsamic or red wine vinegar

2 teaspoons Dijon mustard

2 teaspoons honey mustard

¼ teaspoon salt

⅛ teaspoon dry mustard blended with 1 tablespoon cold water

¼ cup mayonnaise

1 tablespoon minced shallot or red onion

1 Remove and discard any coarse stems from spinach. Then arrange spinach in a wide salad bowl and top with shrimp.

2 In a 1- to 1½-quart pan, combine oil, vinegar, Dijon mustard, honey mustard, salt, and dry mustard mixture. Bring to a boil over medium heat (about 3 minutes), stirring constantly. Remove pan from heat and whisk in mayonnaise and shallot.

3 Pour hot dressing over salad; mix well. Serve immediately.

makes 4 servings

per serving: 417 calories, 26 g protein, 5 g carbohydrates, 33 g total fat, 229 mg cholesterol, 585 mg sodium

sesame-plum pork salad

preparation time: about 15 minutes

1 can (about 8 oz.) crushed pineapple packed in juice, drained well

½ cup prepared Chinese plum sauce

2 tablespoons sugar

1 tablespoon distilled white vinegar

1 teaspoon Asian sesame oil

2 green onions

3 cups shredded purchased Chinese-style barbecued pork or roasted pork

6 cups shredded napa cabbage

½ cup lightly packed cilantro leaves

Lime wedges

1 In a large bowl, stir together pineapple, plum sauce, sugar, vinegar, and oil; set aside.

2 Cut onions into 1½-inch lengths; then cut each piece lengthwise into thin shreds. Add onions and pork to sauce mixture; mix well.

3 Arrange cabbage on a rimmed platter; sprinkle evenly with cilantro. Top with pork mixture. Offer lime wedges to season individual servings to taste.

makes 4 servings

per serving: 322 calories, 22 g protein, 28 g carbohydrates, 15 g total fat, 50 mg cholesterol, 1,122 mg sodium

stir-fried napa cabbage salad

preparation time: about 15 minutes

2 tablespoons unseasoned rice vinegar
   or white wine vinegar

2 tablespoons sugar

1 tablespoon soy sauce

¼ teaspoon ground red pepper (cayenne)

1 medium-size head napa cabbage

3 tablespoons salad oil

1 Stir together vinegar, sugar, soy sauce, and red pepper; set aside.

2 Discard any wilted outer leaves from cabbage. Then rinse cabbage; cut off and discard base. Slice cabbage in half lengthwise and chop coarsely.

3 Heat oil in a wide frying pan or wok over high heat; add cabbage and cook, stirring, until it begins to wilt (2 to 3 minutes). Add vinegar mixture, stir well, and remove from heat. Transfer salad to a serving dish.

makes 4 to 6 servings

per serving: 113 calories, 2 g protein, 9 g carbohydrates, 8 g total fat, 0 mg cholesterol, 216 mg sodium

italian-style vermicelli salad

preparation time: 30 to 35 minutes

8 ounces dry vermicelli or spaghetti

1 jar (8 oz.) marinated artichoke hearts

⅓ cup olive oil or salad oil

2 tablespoons white wine vinegar

1 teaspoon *each* dry oregano and dry basil

¼ teaspoon *each* dry rosemary and pepper

2 cloves garlic, minced or pressed

1½ teaspoons dry mustard

1 medium-size carrot, finely diced

1 small zucchini, finely diced

1 package (3 oz.) sliced salami,
   cut into julienne strips

2 cups shredded mozzarella cheese

⅓ cup grated Parmesan cheese

Lettuce leaves, rinsed and crisped

1 In a 5- to 6-quart pan, cook vermicelli in about 3 quarts boiling water just until al dente (10 to 12 minutes); or cook according to package directions. Drain thoroughly, rinse with cold water, and drain again.

2 Drain marinade from artichokes into a large bowl; chop artichokes and set aside. To marinade, add oil, vinegar, oregano, basil, rosemary, pepper, garlic, mustard, and vermicelli. Stir to coat pasta thoroughly. Add carrot, zucchini, salami, mozzarella cheese, Parmesan cheese, and artichokes. Stir well. Line a platter with lettuce leaves and spoon pasta mixture into center. Serve at room temperature.

makes 6 servings

per serving: 472 calories, 18 g protein, 34 g carbohydrates, 29 g total fat, 44 mg cholesterol, 640 mg sodium

egg salad boats

preparation time: about 15 minutes

12 **hard-cooked eggs, coarsely chopped**

½ **cup mayonnaise**

1 **cup thinly sliced celery**

3 **green onions (including tops), thinly sliced**

¾ **teaspoon dry dill weed**

½ **teaspoon lemon juice**

6 **large tomatoes**

Lettuce leaves, rinsed and crisped

1 In a large bowl, gently stir together eggs, mayonnaise, celery, onions, dill weed, and lemon juice until well combined; set aside. Core tomatoes; then cut each tomato almost to the base into 8 wedges (don't slice all the way through).

2 Place each tomato on a lettuce-lined plate, carefully spread wedges open, and spoon egg salad into center.

makes 6 servings

per serving: 320 calories, 14 g protein, 9 g carbohydrates, 26 g total fat, 436 mg cholesterol, 258 mg sodium

shrimp-rice salad

preparation time: about 20 minutes

½ **cup sliced almonds**

Creamy Lemon Dressing (recipe follows)

3 **cups cold cooked long-grain white rice**

1 **pound small cooked shrimp**

1 **cup** *each* **thinly diced celery and chopped green bell pepper**

1 **can (about 8 oz.) sliced water chestnuts, drained**

Salt and pepper

Lettuce leaves, rinsed and crisped

1 Spread almonds in a shallow baking pan and toast in a 350° oven, stirring occasionally, until golden (about 6 minutes). Meanwhile, prepare Creamy Lemon Dressing.

2 In a large bowl, gently stir together rice, shrimp, celery, bell pepper, and water chestnuts; add dressing and stir gently until all ingredients are well coated. Season to taste with salt and pepper. Line a platter or 4 individual plates with lettuce leaves; spoon salad atop lettuce and top with almonds.

CREAMY LEMON DRESSING

Mix ¾ cup mayonnaise, 1 teaspoon grated lemon peel, 1 tablespoon lemon juice, 2 teaspoons prepared horseradish, and ¼ teaspoon garlic powder. Then stir in ½ cup thinly sliced green onions (including tops), ¼ cup chopped parsley, and 1 jar (2 oz.) sliced pimientos (drained).

makes 4 servings

per serving: 696 calories, 31 g protein, 52 g carbohydrates, 41 g total fat, 246 mg cholesterol, 533 mg sodium

hunan lamb on cool greens

preparation time: 30 minutes

2 tablespoons seasoned rice vinegar

1 tablespoon soy sauce

2 teaspoons Asian sesame oil

1 teaspoon lemon juice

1 tablespoon cornstarch

3 tablespoons hoisin sauce

2 tablespoons chili paste with garlic

1 tablespoon sugar

12 cups mixed salad greens, rinsed and crisped

1 medium-size cucumber, halved
   and thinly sliced

⅔ cup lightly packed cilantro leaves

1 tablespoon vegetable oil

1 large onion, halved and thinly sliced

1 pound lean boneless leg of lamb, trimmed
   of fat and cut into ¾-inch cubes

1 Chili lovers will enjoy this dish of quick-cooked lamb cloaked in a spicy-hot dressing and served with plenty of crisp greens and cucumber. For even more fiery flavor, offer hot chili oil to add at the table.

2 In a small bowl, whisk vinegar, soy sauce, sesame oil, and lemon juice to blend. Add cornstarch; stir until smoothly blended. Add hoisin sauce, chili paste, and sugar; blend well. Set aside.

3 In a large serving bowl, mix greens, cucumber, and two-thirds of the cilantro.

4 Heat vegetable oil in a wide nonstick frying pan over medium-high heat. Add onion and cook, stirring often, until soft (about 5 minutes); add water, 1 tablespoon at a time, if pan appears dry. Add lamb and cook, stirring often, until done to your liking; cut in thickest part to test (2 to 3 minutes for medium-rare).

5 Stir hoisin mixture and pour into pan. Cook, stirring, until sauce boils and thickens slightly (1 to 2 minutes). Immediately spoon lamb mixture over greens. Sprinkle with remaining cilantro.

makes 4 servings

per serving: 307 calories, 25 g protein, 23 g carbohydrates, 11 g total fat, 73 mg cholesterol, 939 mg sodium

cherry tomatoes & onions vinaigrette

preparation time: about 15 minutes

¼ cup olive oil or salad oil

⅓ cup red wine vinegar

1 small clove garlic, minced or pressed

1 tablespoon finely chopped fresh oregano
   or 1 teaspoon dry oregano

7 to 8 cups cherry tomatoes, halved

1 medium-size mild white onion, thinly sliced

Salt and pepper

In a large salad bowl, whisk together oil, vinegar, garlic, and oregano. Then add tomatoes and onion; mix gently to coat well. Season to taste with salt and pepper.

makes 6 to 8 servings

per serving: 95 calories, 1 g protein, 6 g carbohydrates, 8 g total fat, 0 mg cholesterol, 9 mg sodium

broiled avocado salad

preparation time: about 20 minutes

Caesar Dressing (recipe follows)

3 medium-size ripe avocados

4 teaspoons grated Parmesan cheese

½ pound small cooked shrimp

¼ cup shredded jack cheese

Salt

1 Prepare Caesar Dressing; set aside.

2 Halve and pit avocados. With a small, sharp knife, score avocado flesh lengthwise and cross-wise just to shells (not through them), making cuts about ½ inch apart.

3 Mix Parmesan cheese, shrimp, and dressing; mound mixture into cavities of avocados. Arrange avocados in an 8- or 9-inch-square baking pan. Sprinkle filling with jack cheese.

4 Broil about 4 inches below heat until jack cheese is melted and avocados are partially warmed (5 to 6 minutes). Season to taste with salt and serve hot.

CAESAR DRESSING

Mix ¼ cup salad oil, 3 tablespoons red wine vinegar, 1 tablespoon lemon juice, 2 teaspoons Dijon mustard, 1 teaspoon anchovy paste or drained, minced canned anchovies, and ¼ teaspoon pepper.

makes 6 servings

per serving: 307 calories, 12 g protein, 8 g carbohydrates, 27 g total fat, 79 mg cholesterol, 216 mg sodium

vegetable cottage cheese salad

preparation time: about 30 minutes

2 cups small-curd cottage cheese

2 tablespoons chopped parsley

½ cup thinly sliced green onions (including tops)

¼ cup chopped green or red bell pepper

⅓ cup chopped celery

½ cup *each* chopped radishes and shredded carrot

½ teaspoon *each* garlic salt, dry dill weed, and dry mustard

2 red or green bell peppers

Spinach or lettuce leaves, rinsed and crisped

Paprika

2 hard-cooked eggs, cut into wedges

1 Combine cottage cheese, parsley, onions, chopped bell pepper, celery, radishes, carrot, garlic salt, dill weed, and mustard; mix lightly. Cover and refrigerate.

2 Cut bell peppers into halves; discard seeds. Line 4 salad plates with spinach. Mound cottage cheese mixture in peppers. Place a stuffed pepper half on each plate and sprinkle lightly with paprika. Garnish with eggs.

makes 4 servings

per serving: 175 calories, 17 g protein, 9 g carbohydrates, 8 g total fat, 122 mg cholesterol, 713 mg sodium

tuscan bread & bean salad

preparation time: 15 minutes

8 to 12 large butter lettuce leaves, rinsed and crisped

½ cup balsamic vinegar

¼ cup olive oil

1 tablespoon honey

2 tablespoons chopped fresh thyme (or to taste)

2 tablespoons thinly sliced green onion

⅛ teaspoon crushed red pepper flakes

2 cans (about 15 oz. *each*) cannellini (white kidney beans), rinsed and drained

2 large tomatoes, chopped and drained well

4 cups purchased plain or seasoned croutons

1 Line 4 shallow individual bowls with lettuce leaves.

2 In a large bowl, whisk vinegar, oil, honey, thyme, onion, and red pepper flakes to blend. Add beans and tomatoes; mix gently but thoroughly. Mix in croutons. Spoon bean mixture into lettuce-lined bowls.

makes 4 servings

per serving: 455 calories, 13 g protein, 63 g carbohydrates, 17 g total fat, 0 mg cholesterol, 665 mg sodium

minted lentils with goat cheese

preparation time: 30 minutes

1¾ cups lentils

3 cups vegetable broth

½ teaspoon dill seeds

1 teaspoon dried thyme

3 tablespoons red wine vinegar

2 to 3 tablespoons olive oil

Red cabbage leaves, rinsed and crisped (optional)

½ cup thinly sliced red onion

About 4 ounces goat cheese, such as Montrachet or bûcheron, coarsely crumbled

¼ cup chopped fresh mint

Mint sprigs (optional)

1 Sort through lentils, discarding any debris. Rinse and drain lentils; place in a 2- to 3-quart pan and add broth, dill seeds, and thyme. Bring to a boil over high heat. Reduce heat, cover, and simmer, stirring once or twice, just until lentils are tender to bite (15 to 20 minutes). Drain, reserving liquid. Transfer lentils to a wide, shallow bowl and let cool for 5 minutes, stirring occasionally.

2 To lentils, add 4 to 6 tablespoons of the reserved cooking liquid (just enough to moisten); then add vinegar and 1 tablespoon of the oil.

3 Line a platter or individual plates with cabbage leaves, if desired; then spoon lentil mixture onto platter. Top with onion, cheese, and chopped mint; drizzle with 1 to 2 tablespoons more oil. Garnish with mint sprigs, if desired.

makes 4 to 6 servings

per serving: 392 calories, 24 g protein, 43 g carbohydrates, 15 g total fat, 18 mg cholesterol, 724 mg sodium

radicchio cups with shrimp & dill

preparation time: about 20 minutes

1 head radicchio (4 to 5 inches in diameter)

1 to 2 tablespoons slivered Black Forest ham, Westphalian ham, or prosciutto

⅓ cup olive oil or salad oil

1 pound small cooked shrimp

2 tablespoons red wine vinegar

1½ tablespoons chopped fresh dill or 2½ teaspoons dry dill weed

Salt and pepper

Dill sprigs (optional)

PREPARING SALAD GREENS Putting salads together is simpler if you rinse and crisp the greens in advance. First discard the coarse outer leaves and stems; then rinse the remaining leaves and dry them in a lettuce spinner (or drain on paper towels or a clean dishtowel). Wrap the leaves loosely in dry paper towels; store in a plastic bag in the crisper of your refrigerator.

1 Remove 4 large outer leaves from radicchio (reserve remainder of head for other uses). Rinse leaves, wrap in paper towels, and refrigerate.

2 In a small frying pan, stir ham and oil over low heat until oil picks up ham flavor (about 5 minutes). Transfer to a medium-size bowl; stir until cool. Stir in shrimp, vinegar, and chopped dill. Season to taste with salt and pepper.

3 Place a radicchio leaf on each of 4 dinner plates. Spoon shrimp mixture equally into center of each leaf. Garnish with dill sprigs, if desired.

makes 4 servings

per serving: 284 calories, 25 g protein, 2 g carbohydrates, 19 g total fat, 223 mg cholesterol, 309 mg sodium

tuna chutney salad

preparation time: about 20 minutes

½ cup mayonnaise

⅓ cup finely chopped Major Grey's chutney

1 teaspoon curry powder

1 tablespoon white wine vinegar

¼ teaspoon ground ginger

8 cups bite-size pieces spinach, red leaf lettuce, butter lettuce, or romaine lettuce (or a combination), rinsed and crisped

2 cups thinly sliced celery

½ cup thinly sliced green onions (including tops)

1 can (about 8 oz.) pineapple chunks in their own juice, drained

2 cans (6⅛ oz. *each*) chunk light tuna in water, drained and flaked; or 2 to 3 cups diced cooked chicken or turkey

⅔ cup Spanish peanuts

In a small bowl, stir together mayonnaise, chutney, curry powder, vinegar, and ginger; set aside. In a large salad bowl, combine greens, celery, onions, pineapple, and tuna. Just before serving, pour dressing over salad and toss to coat greens thoroughly; sprinkle peanuts over top.

makes 4 to 6 servings

per serving: 456 calories, 28 g protein, 27 g carbohydrates, 28 g total fat, 41 mg cholesterol, 546 mg sodium

salade niçoise for two

preparation time: 30 to 35 minutes

4 small thin-skinned potatoes (*each* 1½ to 2 inches in diameter), scrubbed ¼ pound green beans, ends removed

Spinach leaves, rinsed and crisped

2 cans (3½ oz. *each*) solid light tuna in water, drained

4 anchovy fillets

Pitted ripe olives or Niçoise olives

2 hard-cooked eggs, cut into quarters

¼ cup olive oil or salad oil

2 tablespoons red wine vinegar

1 clove garlic, minced or pressed

½ teaspoon Dijon mustard

Dash *each* of salt and pepper

1 Place unpeeled potatoes in a 2-quart pan; add water to cover. Bring to a boil over high heat; cover and boil for 15 minutes. Add beans and continue to boil until potatoes are tender throughout when pierced and beans are just tender-crisp to bite (about 6 more minutes). Drain vegetables and rinse under cold running water until cool enough to handle; drain again. Peel potatoes, if desired; then cut into ¼-inch-thick slices.

2 Line 2 salad plates with spinach leaves. Invert one can of tuna onto each plate; arrange anchovies in a crisscross pattern over tuna. Arrange potatoes, beans, olives, and eggs around tuna.

3 In a small bowl, stir together oil, vinegar, garlic, mustard, salt, and pepper. Drizzle dressing evenly over salads.

makes 2 servings

per serving: 562 calories, 38 g protein, 26 g carbohydrates, 34 g total fat, 254 mg cholesterol, 785 mg sodium

san diego salad

preparation time: about 25 minutes

Creamy Cumin Dressing (recipe follows)

1 head romaine lettuce, separated into leaves, rinsed, and crisped

About 3 cups bite-size pieces cooked chicken breast

3 to 4 ounces jack cheese, cut into bite-size strips

12 thin slices salami

2 oranges, peeled and sliced

1 firm-ripe avocado

Pitted ripe olives

Tortilla chips

1 Prepare Creamy Cumin Dressing; set aside.

2 Arrange large outer lettuce leaves on 4 dinner plates. Finely chop inner leaves and arrange over whole leaves. Top with chicken, cheese, salami, and orange slices. Pit, peel, and slice avocado; add to salads. Garnish with olives and tortilla chips. Offer dressing at the table to add to taste.

makes 4 servings

CREAMY CUMIN DRESSING

Mix ⅓ cup *each* sour cream and mayonnaise, 1½ tablespoons lemon juice, ¼ teaspoon *each* dry mustard and garlic salt, ½ teaspoon ground cumin, and 3 tablespoons prepared green or red Chile salsa.

makes about 1 cup

per serving of salad: 498 calories, 48 g protein, 16 g carbohydrates, 27 g total fat, 130 mg cholesterol, 625 mg sodium

per tablespoon of dressing: 44 calories, 0.2 g protein, 0.6 g carbohydrates, 5 g total fat, 5 mg cholesterol, 74 mg sodium

curry & fruit chicken salad

preparation time: about 30 minutes

Dill-Curry Dressing (recipe follows)

1 medium-size red apple

3 cups ½-inch-wide strips of cooked chicken

2 cups thinly sliced celery

¾ cup salted roasted peanuts

½ cup raisins

1 small pineapple

8 to 10 large lettuce leaves, rinsed and crisped

2 tablespoons minced candied or crystallized ginger (optional)

1 Prepare Dill-Curry Dressing; set aside.

2 Core apple and cut lengthwise into thin slivers. Combine apple, chicken, celery, ½ cup of the peanuts, raisins, and dressing; mix gently.

3 Peel and slice pineapple. Arrange lettuce leaves on 4 dinner plates; place pineapple on lettuce and top with chicken salad. Sprinkle salads with remaining ¼ cup peanuts and, if desired, ginger.

DILL-CURRY DRESSING

Mix 1 cup sour cream or plain yogurt, 2 tablespoons lemon juice, 1 ½ teaspoons curry powder, and ½ teaspoon dry dill weed.

makes 4 servings

per serving: 656 calories, 41 g protein, 54 g carbohydrates, 34 g total fat, 119 mg cholesterol, 421 mg sodium

chicken salad with sesame dressing

preparation time: about 30 minutes

Sesame Dressing (recipe follows)

8 cups bite-size pieces leaf lettuce, rinsed and crisped

4 large kiwi fruit

1 large firm-ripe avocado

2 cups shredded cooked chicken

1 cup thinly sliced celery

⅓ cup thinly sliced green onions (including tops)

1 Prepare Sesame Dressing; set aside.

2 Spread lettuce in a wide salad bowl. Peel kiwi fruit and thinly slice crosswise. Pit, peel, and slice avocado. Arrange kiwi fruit, avocado, chicken, celery, and onions over lettuce. Pour dressing over salad and mix lightly.

SESAME DRESSING

Heat ⅓ cup salad oil in a small frying pan over low heat. Add 3 tablespoons sesame seeds and cook, stirring often, until golden (about 5 minutes). Remove from heat and let cool for 10 minutes. Stir in ½ teaspoon *each* grated lemon peel and dry mustard, ¼ cup lemon juice, and 1 tablespoon *each* sugar and soy sauce. Season to taste with salt.

makes 4 servings

per serving: 545 calories, 27 g protein, 32 g carbohydrates, 37 g total fat, 62 mg cholesterol, 374 mg sodium

smoked chicken breast salad

preparation time: about 35 to 40 minutes

3 tablespoons liquid smoke

2 whole chicken breasts (about 1 lb. *each*), skinned, boned, and split

Orange Vinaigrette (recipe follows)

1 tablespoon butter or margarine

¾ cup pecan halves

6 cups mixed salad greens, such as butter lettuce, romaine lettuce, and watercress, rinsed and crisped

Orange zest

Orange wedges

1 Pour liquid smoke into a 5- to 6-quart pan. Set a rack in pan. Arrange chicken breasts in a single layer on rack and cover pan tightly. Bake in a 350° oven until meat in thickest part is no longer pink; cut to test (20 to 25 minutes). If made ahead, let cool; then cover and refrigerate for up to 2 days.

2 While chicken is baking, prepare Orange Vinaigrette; set aside. Also melt butter in a medium-size frying pan over low heat. Add pecans and stir until nuts are slightly darkened and have a toasted flavor (about 6 minutes). Drain on paper towels.

3 Arrange salad greens on 4 dinner plates and sprinkle with pecans. Cut each chicken breast into ¼-inch-thick slanting slices; arrange on plates beside greens. Spoon Orange Vinaigrette over greens and chicken. Garnish with orange zest and orange wedges.

ORANGE VINAIGRETTE

Mix ¼ cup orange juice, 2 tablespoons *each* white wine vinegar and salad oil, 1 tablespoon thinly slivered or shredded orange peel, 2 teaspoons *each* honey and Dijon mustard, and ½ teaspoon coarsely ground pepper.

makes 4 servings

per serving: 420 calories, 37 g protein, 12 g carbohydrates, 25 g total fat, 93 mg cholesterol, 213 mg sodium

curried turkey salad with papaya

preparation time: about 25 minutes

Curry Dressing (recipe follows)

3 cups diced cooked turkey or chicken

1 cup thinly sliced celery

½ cup thinly sliced green onions (including tops)

Salt and ground red pepper (cayenne)

8 to 12 large romaine lettuce leaves, rinsed and crisped

2 large papayas, peeled, seeded, and sliced lengthwise

¼ cup salted roasted cashews

1 lemon, cut into wedges

1 Prepare Curry Dressing; set aside.

2 Combine turkey, celery, and onions; mix lightly with dressing. Season to taste with salt and red pepper.

3 Arrange lettuce on 4 dinner plates. Mound turkey salad on each plate; arrange papaya slices alongside. Sprinkle cashews over salad. Offer lemon wedges to squeeze over salad and fruit.

CURRY DRESSING

Mix 1 cup sour cream; 2 tablespoons minced candied or crystallized ginger; 1 tablespoon *each* curry powder, lemon juice, and Dijon mustard; and ½ teaspoon cumin seeds.

makes 4 servings

per serving: 473 calories, 36 g protein, 35 g carbohydrates, 22 g total fat, 106 mg cholesterol, 314 mg sodium

green salad with roasted peppers

preparation time: about 30 minutes

1 cup canned roasted red peppers

About ¼ cup extra-virgin olive oil

About 3 tablespoons balsamic vinegar

1 clove garlic, minced

10 to 12 niçoise or calamata olives

8 to 12 baguette slices

½ cup thinly sliced mild red onion

10 cups spinach leaves, rinsed and drained

2 cups frisée or curly endive, rinsed and drained

Salt

⅓ cup fresh-grated Parmesan cheese

1 Cut peppers into ¼-inch-wide strips and put in a wide salad bowl. Add 1 teaspoon olive oil, 3 tablespoons vinegar, garlic, and olives; mix.

2 Brush baguette slices lightly on 1 side with olive oil (about 1 tablespoon total). Lay oiled side up in a 10- by 15-inch pan. Bake in a 375° oven until lightly toasted, about 8 minutes; cool on a rack.

3 To bowl, add onion, spinach, and frisée; mix, and season to taste with more vinegar and salt.

4 Heat 2 tablespoons oil in a 6- to 8-inch frying pan over high heat, about 1 minute. Pour over salad and mix. Add cheese and baguette slices; mix again.

makes 6 to 8 servings

per serving: 137 calories., 4.1 g protein, 11 g carbohydrates, 9.2 g total fat, 3.2 mg cholesterol, 231 mg sodium

arugula salad with goat cheese medallions

preparation time: 20 to 25 minutes

⅓ cup pine nuts

⅓ cup currants

3 tablespoons extra-virgin olive oil

1 tablespoon white wine vinegar

9 to 10 ounces small, tender arugula leaves or salad mix, rinsed and drained

1 to 3 logs (11 to 12 oz. *total*) fresh chèvre (goat) cheese, cut into 8 to 10 equal rounds

Salt and pepper

1 In an 8- to 10-inch nonstick frying pan over medium-high heat, stir nuts often until golden, 3 to 4 minutes. Add currants, stir, and pour mixture into a small bowl.

2 In a wide bowl, mix 2 tablespoons oil and the vinegar. Add arugula leaves and mix to coat. Mound equal portions on salad plates.

3 Pour 1 tablespoon oil into the frying pan and set over medium-high heat. Lay cheese in pan and heat just until warm, turning once with a wide spatula, ¾ to 1 minute total. Set a portion of cheese on each salad. Sprinkle with nuts and currants. Season to taste with salt and pepper.

makes 8 to 10 servings

per serving: 164 calories., 7.8 g protein, 5.4 g carbohydrates, 13 g total fat, 14 mg cholesterol, 122 mg sodium

mediterranean wheat berry salad

preparation time: about 1 hour

¾ **cup wheat berries**

¾ **cup long-grain brown rice**

1 jar (6 oz.) marinated artichoke hearts

6 tablespoons balsamic or red wine vinegar

2 tablespoons olive oil

2 teaspoons Dijon mustard

1 teaspoon dried oregano

2 Roma tomatoes, rinsed, cored, and cut into ½-inch cubes

1 cucumber, rinsed and cut into ½-inch cubes

¾ **cup thinly sliced green onions**

½ **cup crumbled feta cheese**

⅓ **cup calamata olives, pitted and halved**

⅓ **cup chopped fresh mint leaves**

¼ **cup chopped parsley**

Salt and pepper

1 In a 3- to 4-quart pan, combine wheat berries, rice, and 6 cups water. Bring to a boil over high heat. Cover and simmer until grains are tender to bite, 30 to 35 minutes. Drain. Pour into a large bowl.

2 Drain artichoke marinade into bowl with grains. Coarsely chop artichokes and add to bowl along with vinegar, oil, mustard, and oregano. Mix well and let stand until cool, about 20 minutes.

3 Add tomatoes, cucumber, onions, cheese, olives, mint, and parsley; mix well. Add salt and pepper to taste.

makes 9 servings

per serving: 207 calories, 5.4 g protein, 29 g carbohydrates, 8.3 g total fat, 6.7 mg cholesterol 304 mg sodium

soft-ripened goat cheese and walnut salad

preparation time: about 20 minutes

½ **cup walnut halves or pieces**

2 tablespoons walnut oil

1 tablespoon lemon juice

2 quarts salad mix, rinsed and crisped

Salt and pepper

4 to 6 ounces soft-ripened goat cheese such as Bermuda Triangle or Humboldt Fog

1 Bake walnuts in an 8- or 9-inch pan in a 400° oven until golden, 5 to 8 minutes (about 4 minutes in a convection oven).

2 In a large bowl, combine oil and lemon juice. Add salad mix and stir, adding salt and pepper to taste. With 2 large spoons, divide salad equally among plates.

3 Cut cheese into thin slices and divide evenly among salads. Sprinkle evenly with walnuts.

makes 4 servings

per serving: 226 calories, 7.4 g protein, 4 g carbohydrates, 21 g fat, 13 mg cholesterol, 113 mg sodium

chicken caesar

preparation time: about 35 minutes

½ cup grated Parmesan cheese

¼ teaspoon pepper

¼ teaspoon salt

4 boneless, skinless chicken breast halves
(about 6 oz. *each*)

¼ cup olive oil

2 tablespoons lemon juice

½ teaspoon anchovy paste

½ teaspoon Dijon mustard

1 clove garlic, minced or pressed

12 cups bite-size pieces romaine lettuce,
rinsed and crisped

2 cups purchased plain or seasoned croutons

Lemon slices (optional)

1 In a shallow bowl, combine ¼ cup of the cheese, pepper, and salt. Rinse chicken and pat dry. Turn each piece in cheese mixture to coat completely. Pat any remaining coating on chicken.

2 Arrange chicken in a lightly oiled 9- by 13-inch baking pan. Bake in a 450° oven until meat in thickest part is no longer pink; cut to test (15 to 17 minutes). Let cool slightly.

3 Meanwhile, in a large bowl, whisk oil, lemon juice, anchovy paste, mustard, and garlic to blend. Add lettuce, remaining ¼ cup cheese, and croutons; toss to coat. Divide salad among 4 individual plates.

4 Cut each chicken breast diagonally into 5 strips; carefully arrange one sliced breast atop each salad. Garnish with lemon slices, if desired.

makes 4 servings

per serving: 440 calories, 47 g protein, 14 g carbohydrates, 21 g total fat, 107 mg cholesterol, 586 mg sodium

olive-pecan chicken slaw

preparation time: about 15 minutes

1 tablespoon butter or margarine

½ cup pecan halves

½ cup mayonnaise

2 tablespoons lemon juice

1 teaspoon Dijon mustard

½ teaspoon sugar

¼ teaspoon pepper

1 medium-size Red Delicious apple,
cored and diced

2 cups shredded cabbage

1 ½ cups shredded cooked chicken

1 jar (about 2 oz.) diced pimentos, drained

1 can (about 2 ¼ oz.) sliced ripe olives, drained

¼ cup thinly sliced celery

Salt

1 Melt butter in a small frying pan over medium heat. Add pecans and stir occasionally until nuts are a darker brown (about 5 minutes). Drain on paper towels.

2 While nuts are toasting, combine mayonnaise, lemon juice, mustard, sugar, and pepper in a large bowl. Beat to blend smoothly.

3 To dressing, add apple, cabbage, chicken, pimentos, olives, and celery; mix well. Season to taste with salt; sprinkle with pecans.

makes 4 servings

per serving: 472 calories, 17 g protein, 14 g carbohydrates, 40 g total fat, 71 mg cholesterol, 416 mg sodium

grecian chicken salad plates

preparation time: about 30 minutes

1 jar (6 oz.) marinated artichoke hearts

1 teaspoon grated lemon peel

1 tablespoon lemon juice

1 clove garlic, minced or pressed

½ teaspoon dry oregano

2 tablespoons chopped fresh mint
  or 2 teaspoons dry mint

3 tablespoons olive oil

1 tablespoon drained capers

1 small cucumber

1 head romaine lettuce, separated into leaves,
  rinsed, and crisped

2 cups cherry tomatoes, cut in half

1 yellow or green bell pepper, seeded and cut
  into thin strips

1 cooked (rotisseried or barbecued) chicken
  (2 to 2 ½ lbs.), cut into quarters

2 to 3 ounces feta cheese, crumbled

Greek olives

1 small can (6½ oz.) stuffed grape leaves,
  drained

1 Drain artichokes, reserving marinade in a small bowl; set artichokes aside. To marinade, add lemon peel, lemon juice, garlic, oregano, and mint; whisk in oil until well combined. Stir in capers. Set dressing aside.

2 Peel cucumber and cut in half lengthwise, then scoop out and discard seeds. Slice each cucumber half crosswise into ⅛-inch-thick slices. Set aside large outer lettuce leaves; tear inner leaves into bitesize pieces.

3 Combine cucumber, torn lettuce leaves, tomatoes, bell pepper, and artichokes. Reserve 2 tablespoons of the dressing; mix salad lightly with remaining dressing.

4 Coarsely sliver large lettuce leaves and arrange on 4 dinner plates. Place a chicken quarter on one side of each plate; mound salad mixture on other side. Sprinkle salads with cheese. Drizzle chicken with reserved dressing and garnish each salad with olives and stuffed grape leaves.

makes 4 servings

per serving: 499 calories, 38 g protein, 14 g carbohydrates, 33 g total fat, 115 mg cholesterol, 646 mg sodium

warm spinach salad

preparation time: about 30 minutes

1 package (10 oz.) washed spinach leaves

¼ pound turkey bacon, chopped

1 cup finely chopped red onion

1 package (10 oz.) frozen corn kernels

½ cup red wine vinegar

4 teaspoons sugar

¼ cup crumbled blue cheese

2 cups purchased fat-free croutons

1 If desired, stack spinach leaves and cut into ½-inch-wide strips. Mound spinach equally onto plates.

2 In a 10- to 12-inch nonstick frying pan over high heat, stir turkey bacon until browned and crisp, about 5 minutes. Spoon equal portions of the bacon over spinach.

3 To pan, add onion, corn, vinegar, and sugar. Stir mixture until onion is limp, 3 to 4 minutes. With a slotted spoon, transfer onion and corn onto spinach, then spoon cooking liquid over salads.

4 Arrange blue cheese equally on salads and add croutons.

makes 4 servings

per serving: 265 calories, 12 g protein, 36 g carbohydrates, 8.2 g total fat, 27 mg cholesterol, 721 mg sodium

szechuan chicken salad

preparation time: about 30 minutes

2 tablespoons creamy peanut butter

3 tablespoons soy sauce

¼ cup unseasoned rice vinegar

2 teaspoons sugar

About ¼ teaspoon hot chili oil or ground
   red pepper (cayenne)

2 tablespoons sesame seeds

Salad oil

6 wonton skins (each about 3 inches square),
   cut into ¼-inch-wide strips

8 cups finely shredded iceberg lettuce

2 green onions (including tops), thinly sliced

2 to 3 cups shredded cooked chicken

2 tablespoons chopped fresh cilantro

1 Place peanut butter in a small bowl; with a fork, smoothly mix in soy sauce, a little at a time, until well blended. Stir in vinegar and sugar; season to taste with chili oil.

2 Toast sesame seeds in a small frying pan over medium heat until golden (3 to 5 minutes), shaking pan frequently; set seeds aside. Pour salad oil into pan to a depth of ¼ inch; increase heat to medium-high. When oil is hot, add wonton strips, about half at a time. Cook, stirring, until lightly browned (1½ to 2 minutes). With a slotted spoon, lift out strips and drain on paper towels.

3 Place lettuce in a large salad bowl; top with onions, chicken, and dressing. Sprinkle with sesame seeds, fried wonton strips, and cilantro. Mix lightly.

makes 4 to 6 servings

per serving: 267 calories, 22 g protein, 13 g carbohydrates, 15 g total fat, 50 mg cholesterol, 707 mg sodium

red cabbage & white sausage salad

preparation time: about 25 minutes

¼ cup salad oil

1 to 1¼ pounds white veal sausage, such as
   bratwurst, knockwurst, or wienerwurst,
   cut into ¼-inch-thick slices

3 tablespoons white wine vinegar

2 tablespoons sugar

1½ teaspoons *each* Dijon mustard, celery seeds,
   and Worcestershire

1 clove garlic, minced or pressed

1 cup thinly sliced green onions (including tops)

6 cups finely shredded red cabbage

Salt and pepper

1 Heat oil in a wok or wide frying pan over medium-high heat. Add sausage slices and cook, turning often, until browned.

2 Add vinegar, sugar, mustard, celery seeds, Worcestershire, and garlic; stir until sugar is dissolved. Bring mixture to a boil over high heat; add onions and cabbage, then turn off heat.

3 Lift and turn onions and cabbage with 2 forks or spoons until coated with dressing. Season to taste with salt and pepper. Serve immediately.

makes 6 servings

per serving: 395 calories, 14 g protein, 15 g carbohydrates, 32 g total fat, 51 mg cholesterol, 542 mg sodium

crab salad with avocado dressing

preparation time: about 20 minutes

12 ounces cooked crabmeat

2 medium-size firm-ripe avocados

½ cup sour cream

½ cup lemon juice

⅛ teaspoon ground red pepper (cayenne)

12 cups shredded butter or iceberg lettuce

¼ cup thinly sliced green onions

2 large tomatoes, thinly sliced

Lemon slices

ZESTY SALAD GREENS Each season brings a fresh harvest or crisp greens to tempt salad lovers. Many of the kinds available in markets today are decidedly nippy, so much so that you may want to temper their "bite" by pairing them with other, milder greens. To add variety in color and texture to your salads, sample spicy arugula (also called rocket or roquette), subtly bitter frisée (baby chicory), peppery watercress, mild-flavored mizuna, and red-purple, slightly bitter radicchio.

1 Pick through crab and discard any bits of shell; set aside.

2 Halve and pit avocados; scoop flesh from skins into a blender or food processor. Add sour cream, lemon juice, and red pepper. Whirl until smoothly puréed.

3 In a large bowl, combine lettuce and onions.

4 Divide avocado dressing among 4 wide, shallow individual plates; spread dressing out to rims of plates. Mound lettuce mixture equally on plates; top equally with tomatoes, then with crab. Garnish with lemon slices.

makes 4 servings

per serving: 291 calories, 21 g protein, 6 g saturated fat, 15 g carbohydrates, 18 g total fat, 98 mg cholestorol, 280 mg sodium

smoked salmon & cheese salad

preparation time: about 15 minutes

5 tablespoons olive oil

3 tablespoons white wine vinegar

1 teaspoon Dijon mustard

3 ounces thinly sliced smoked salmon,
   cut into ½-inch-wide strips

⅔ cup crumbled Gorgonzola cheese

1½ cups purchased plain or seasoned croutons

12 cups bite-size pieces romaine lettuce,
   rinsed and crisped

⅓ cup thinly sliced green onions

¼ cup salted roasted almonds,
   coarsely chopped

1 In a large bowl, whisk oil, vinegar, and mustard to blend.

2 To dressing, add salmon, cheese, croutons, lettuce, and onions. Mix well. Sprinkle with almonds.

makes 4 servings

per serving: 372 calories, 13 g protein, 12 g carbohydrates, 31 g total fat, 24 mg cholesterol, 651 mg sodium

steak salad with horseradish dressing

preparation time: 30 minutes

1 flank steak (about 1 lb.)

Salt

½ cup sour cream

½ cup mayonnaise

1 tablespoon prepared horseradish (or to taste)

1 tablespoon lemon juice

⅛ teaspoon pepper

½ cup crumbled blue-veined cheese

12 cups bite-size pieces romaine lettuce, rinsed and crisped

1 large tomato, cut into wedges

1 jar (about 6¼ oz.) marinated artichoke hearts, quartered and drained well

¼ cup thinly sliced red onion

About 1 teaspoon finely shredded lemon peel

1 Place steak on a lightly oiled rack in a broiler pan; sprinkle with salt. Broil about 6 inches below heat, turning once, until well browned on both sides and done to your liking; cut in thickest part to test (10 to 14 minutes for medium-rare).

2 Meanwhile, in a small bowl, stir together sour cream, mayonnaise, horseradish, lemon juice, and pepper. Stir in cheese. Set aside.

3 In a large bowl, toss together lettuce, tomato, artichokes, and onion; divide among 4 to 6 individual plates.

4 Cut steak across the grain into thin, slanting slices. Arrange steak over salads. Drizzle salads with dressing and garnish with lemon peel.

makes 4 to 6 servings

per serving: 395 calories, 20 g protein, 8 g carbohydrates, 32 g total fat, 67 mg cholesterol, 542 mg sodium

litchi chicken salad

preparation time: 20 minutes

1 can (about 1 lb.) litchis

½ cup plain nonfat yogurt

½ teaspoon grated lemon peel

1 tablespoon lemon juice

1 teaspoon dried thyme

3 cups bite-size pieces cooked chicken

½ cup finely chopped celery

Salt and pepper

8 large butter lettuce leaves, rinsed and crisped

¼ cup thinly sliced green onions

1 Drain litchis, reserving 2 tablespoons of the syrup; set fruit aside.

2 In a large bowl, stir together reserved 2 tablespoons litchi syrup, yogurt, lemon peel, lemon juice, and thyme. Stir in chicken and celery. Season to taste with salt and pepper.

3 Line 4 individual plates with lettuce leaves; spoon chicken salad equally onto lettuce. Top salads equally with litchis and onions.

makes 4 servings

per serving; 305 calories, 33 g protein, 26 g carbohydrates, 8 g total fat, 94 mg cholesterol, 166 mg sodium

tofu toss with spicy peanut sauce

preparation time: 30 minutes

1 package (about 6 oz.) frozen Chinese
   pea pods, thawed and drained

1 pound firm tofu, rinsed, drained, and
   cut into ½-inch cubes

2 cloves garlic, minced or pressed

⅛ teaspoon ground red pepper (cayenne),
   or to taste

½ cup creamy peanut butter

½ cup hoisin sauce

½ cup seasoned rice vinegar

1 teaspoon Asian sesame oil

1 large head radicchio

6 cups finely shredded napa cabbage

½ cup lightly packed cilantro leaves

¼ cup thinly sliced shallots or red onion

1 tablespoon vegetable oil

Lime wedges

1 Cut pea pods diagonally in half. Transfer to a large bowl and add tofu, garlic, and red pepper; mix gently.

2 In a small bowl, beat peanut butter, hoisin sauce, vinegar, and sesame oil to blend smoothly. Set aside.

3 Remove 8 to 12 large outer leaves from radicchio; rinse and drain well. Arrange leaves, overlapping if necessary, in a wide, shallow bowl. Rinse, drain, and finely shred remaining radicchio; place in a large bowl and mix with cabbage, cilantro, and shallots.

4 Heat vegetable oil in a wide nonstick frying pan over medium-high heat. Add tofu mixture and cook, stirring often, until almost all liquid has evaporated and tofu is heated through (about 5 minutes). Stir in peanut butter mixture. Cook, stirring, just until sauce is heated through (1 to 2 minutes). Pour tofu mixture over cabbage mixture; mix well. Spoon into radicchio-lined bowl. Offer lime wedges to season individual servings to taste.

makes 4 to 6 servings

per serving: 451 calories, 25 g protein, 36 g carbohydrates, 25 g total fat, 0 mg cholesterol, 1,146 mg sodium

carrot salad with peppercorns

preparation time: about 20 minutes

1¼ pounds carrots

2 tablespoons chopped fresh tarragon
   or 2 teaspoons dry tarragon

2 tablespoons canned green peppercorns,
   drained

¼ cup olive oil or salad oil

2 tablespoons lemon juice

Salt and pepper

1 Cut carrots into matchstick-size pieces.

2 In a 3- to 4-quart pan, bring 6 cups water to a boil over high heat. Add carrots and cook until tender-crisp to bite (about 2 minutes). Drain, plunge into ice water, and stir until cool. Then drain again.

3 Place carrots, tarragon, peppercorns, oil, and lemon juice in a serving bowl and mix gently. Season to taste with salt and pepper.

makes 4 servings

per serving: 186 calories, 2 g protein, 16 g carbohydrates, 14 g total fat, 0 mg cholesterol, 48 mg sodium

pesto pasta salad

preparation time: 35 minutes

1 cup dried tomatoes (not packed in oil)

2 tablespoons pine nuts

1 pound dried medium-size pasta shells or elbow macaroni

1 cup firmly packed chopped fresh spinach

3 tablespoons dried basil

1 or 2 cloves garlic, peeled

1/3 cup grated Parmesan cheese

1/4 cup olive oil

1 teaspoon Asian sesame oil

Salt and pepper

1 Place tomatoes in a small bowl and add boiling water to cover. Let stand until soft (about 10 minutes), stirring occasionally. Drain well; gently squeeze out excess liquid. Cut tomatoes into thin slivers and set aside.

2 While tomatoes are soaking, toast pine nuts in a small frying pan over medium heat until golden (about 3 minutes), stirring often. Pour out of pan and set aside.

3 In a 6- to 8-quart pan, bring 4 quarts water to a boil over medium-high heat; stir in pasta and cook until just tender to bite, 8 to 10 minutes. (Or cook pasta according to package directions.) Drain, rinse with cold water until cool, and drain well again. Pour into a large serving bowl.

4 In a food processor or blender, whirl spinach, basil, garlic, cheese, olive oil, sesame oil, and 1 teaspoon water until smoothly puréed; scrape sides of container as needed and add a little more water if pesto is too thick.

5 Add tomatoes and spinach pesto to pasta; mix well. Sprinkle with pine nuts; season to taste with salt and pepper.

makes 8 servings

per serving: 332 calories, 11 g protein, 49 g carbohydrates, 10 g total fat, 3 mg cholesterol, 78 mg sodium

capellini chinese style

preparation time: about 35 minutes
chilling time: at least 30 minutes

3 tablespoons seasoned rice vinegar; or 3 tablespoons distilled white vinegar and 2 teaspoons sugar

3 tablespoons lime juice

4 teaspoons Asian sesame oil (or to taste)

1 tablespoon reduced-sodium soy sauce

1/16 teaspoon ground red pepper (cayenne)

8 ounces dried capellini

1/2 cup thinly sliced green onions

1/3 cup chopped red bell pepper

Lime wedges

1 Combine vinegar, lime juice, oil, soy sauce, and ground red pepper in a large nonmetal serving bowl; mix until blended. Set aside.

2 Bring 8 cups water to a boil in a 4- to 5-quart pan over medium-high heat. Stir in pasta and cook just until tender to bite (about 4 minutes); or cook according to package directions. Drain, rinse with cold water until cool, and drain well.

3 Add pasta to vinegar mixture. Mix thoroughly but gently. Cover and refrigerate until cool (at least 30 minutes) or for up to 4 hours; stir occasionally.

4 Stir in onions and bell pepper just before serving. Offer lime wedges to add to taste.

makes 4 to 6 servings

per serving: 217 calories, 6 g protein, 38 g carbohydrates, 4 g total fat, 0 mg cholesterol, 305 mg sodium

mixed greens with pesto dressing

preparation time: 35 minutes

1 tablespoon pine nuts

2 teaspoons Asian sesame oil

1 clove garlic, minced or pressed

3 slices Italian or sourdough sandwich bread, cut into 1/2-inch cubes

1/4 cup chopped fresh basil

1/4 cup chopped Italian or regular parsley

1 cup nonfat sour cream

1 tablespoon white wine vinegar

1 teaspoon honey

1 or 2 cloves garlic, peeled

Salt and pepper

8 ounces (about 8 cups) mixed salad greens, rinsed and crisped

1 Toast pine nuts in a wide nonstick frying pan over medium heat until golden (about 3 minutes), stirring often. Pour out of pan and set aside. In same pan (with pan off heat), combine 1 teaspoon of the oil, garlic, and 1 tablespoon water. Add bread cubes and toss gently to coat. Place pan over medium heat; cook, stirring occasionally, until croutons are crisp and tinged with brown (about 10 minutes). Remove from pan and set aside.

2 In a food processor or blender, combine basil, parsley, sour cream, vinegar, honey, remaining 1 teaspoon oil, and garlic; whirl until smoothly puréed. Season to taste with salt and pepper; set aside.

3 Place greens in a large bowl; add dressing and mix gently but thoroughly Add croutons and mix again. Sprinkle with pine nuts.

makes 4 servings

per serving: 154 calories, 8 g protein, 20 g carbohydrates, 4 g total fat, 0 mg cholesterol, 177 mg sodium

fennel & orange salad

preparation time: 20 minutes

2 large heads fennel

1/4 cup seasoned rice vinegar

2 tablespoons olive oil

1 tablespoon grated orange peel

1 teaspoon anise seeds

4 large oranges

Seeds from 1 pomegranate

Salt

1 Trim stems from fennel, reserving the feathery green leaves. Trim and discard any bruised areas from fennel; then cut each fennel head into thin slivers. Place slivered fennel in a large bowl.

2 Finely chop enough of the fennel leaves to make 1 tablespoon (reserve remaining leaves); add to bowl along with vinegar, oil, orange peel, and anise seeds. Mix well.

3 Cut off and discard peel and all white membrane from oranges. Cut fruit crosswise into slices about 1/4 inch thick; discard seeds.

4 Divide fennel mixture among individual plates. Arrange oranges alongside fennel mixture; sprinkle salads equally with pomegranate seeds. Garnish with reserved fennel leaves. Season to taste with salt.

makes 6 servings

per serving: 147 calories, 2 g protein, 26 g carbohydrates, 5 g total fat, 0 mg cholesterol, 290 mg sodium

garbanzo antipasto salad

preparation time: about 50 minutes
chilling time: at least 1 hour

8 ounces sourdough bread, cut into about
  ¹/₂-inch cubes

¹/₂ cup white wine vinegar

2 tablespoons olive oil

1 tablespoon chopped fresh oregano or 1 teaspoon
  dried oregano

2 teaspoons honey (or to taste)

2 cloves garlic, minced or pressed

¹/₈ to ¹/₄ teaspoon pepper

2 cans (about 15 oz. *each*) garbanzo beans,
  drained and rinsed

2 large tomatoes, chopped and drained well

¹/₄ cup slivered red onion, in about 1-inch lengths

¹/₄ cup oil-cured olives, pitted and sliced

3 to 4 tablespoons drained capers

¹/₃ cup *each* nonfat mayonnaise and nonfat sour
  cream

2 tablespoons chopped fresh dill or 2 teaspoons
  dried dill weed

8 to 12 butter lettuce leaves, rinsed and crisped

1 Spread bread cubes in a single layer in a shallow 10- by 15-inch baking pan. Bake in a 325° oven, stirring occasionally, until crisp and tinged with brown (15 to 20 minutes). Set aside. If made ahead, let cool completely in pan on a rack, then store airtight for up to 2 days.

2 In a large bowl, combine vinegar, oil, oregano, honey, garlic, and pepper. Beat until blended. Add beans, tomatoes, onion, olives, and capers; mix gently but thoroughly. Cover and refrigerate for at least 1 hour or up to 4 hours.

3 Meanwhile, in a small bowl, beat mayonnaise, sour cream, and dill until smoothly blended; cover and refrigerate.

4 To serve, line 4 individual rimmed plates or shallow bowls with lettuce leaves. Add croutons to salad and mix gently but thoroughly, being sure to coat croutons with marinade. Then, using a slotted spoon, transfer salad to plates; top each serving with a dollop of dill dressing.

makes 4 servings

per serving: 466 calories, 16 g protein, 67 g carbohydrates, 15 g total fat, 0 mg cholesterol, 1,234 mg sodium

green chile dressing

preparation time: about 10 minutes

1 small can (about 4 oz.) diced green chiles

¹/₃ cup lime juice

¹/₄ cup water

¹/₄ cup chopped cilantro

1 clove garlic, peeled

1 or 2 fresh jalapeño chiles, seeded and chopped

1 ¹/₂ teaspoons sugar

In a blender or food processor, combine green chiles, lime juice, water, cilantro, garlic, jalapeño chiles, and sugar; whirl until smoothly puréed. (At this point, you may cover and refrigerate dressing for up to 4 hours.)

makes about 1 cup

per tablespoon: 5 calories, 0.1 g protein, 1 g carbohydrates, 0.01 g total fat, 0 mg cholesterol, 44 mg sodium

steak, couscous & greens with raspberries

preparation time: about 1¼ hours
marinating time: at least 30 minutes
chilling time: at least 30 minutes

1 pound lean boneless top sirloin steak (about 1 inch thick), trimmed of fat

½ cup dry red wine

5 tablespoons raspberry vinegar or red wine vinegar

¼ cup chopped green onions

2 tablespoons reduced-sodium soy sauce

1 tablespoon sugar

2 teaspoons chopped fresh tarragon or ½ teaspoon dried tarragon

1 tablespoon raspberry or apple jelly

¾ cup low-sodium chicken broth

⅔ cup low-fat milk

¼ teaspoon ground coriander

6½ ounces (about 1 cup) dried couscous

1 tablespoon olive oil

8 cups bite-size pieces red leaf lettuce leaves

2 cups raspberries

Tarragon sprigs (optional)

1 Slice steak across grain into strips about ⅛ inch thick and 3 inches long. Place meat, wine, 1 tablespoon of the vinegar, 2 tablespoons of the onions, soy sauce, 2 teaspoons of the sugar, and chopped tarragon in a large heavy-duty resealable plastic bag or large nonmetal bowl. Seal bag and rotate to coat meat (or stir meat in bowl and cover airtight). Refrigerate for at least 30 minutes or up to a day, turning (or stirring) occasionally.

2 Cook jelly in a 2- to 3-quart pan over low heat, stirring, until melted. Add broth, milk, and coriander; increase heat to medium-high and bring to a gentle boil. Stir in couscous. Cover, remove from heat, and let stand until liquid is absorbed (about 5 minutes).

3 Transfer couscous mixture to a large nonmetal bowl; let cool briefly, fluffing occasionally with a fork. Cover and refrigerate until cool (at least 30 minutes) or for up to 2 hours, fluffing occasionally. Meanwhile, heat 1 teaspoon of the oil in a wide nonstick frying pan over medium-high heat. Add meat and its juices and cook, stirring, until browned and done to your liking; cut to test (3 to 5 minutes). Transfer to a large nonmetal bowl and let cool.

4 Combine remaining 2 teaspoons oil, remaining 4 tablespoons vinegar, and remaining 1 teaspoon sugar in a large nonmetal bowl. Mix until blended. Add lettuce and turn to coat. Arrange lettuce on individual plates. Stir remaining 2 tablespoons onions into couscous mixture. Spoon onto lettuce, top with meat, and sprinkle with raspberries. Garnish with tarragon sprigs, if desired.

makes 4 servings

per serving: 456 calories, 34 g protein, 55 g carbohydrates, 10 g total fat, 71 mg cholesterol, 273 mg sodium

creamy herb dressing

1 cup plain nonfat yogurt

3 tablespoons balsamic vinegar

1½ teaspoons chopped fresh oregano or ¼ teaspoon dried oregano

1 teaspoon Dijon mustard

2 to 3 teaspoons sugar

In a nonmetal bowl, mix yogurt, vinegar, oregano, mustard, and sugar. If made ahead, cover and refrigerate for up to 3 days.

makes 1¼ cups

per tablespoon: 9 calories, 0.6 g protein, 1 g carbohydrates, 0 g total fat, 0.2 mg cholesterol, 15 mg sodium

orange & olive patio salad

preparation time: about 20 minutes
cooling time: about 1 hour

½ cup water

1 teaspoon arrowroot

4 teaspoons honey

2 tablespoons finely chopped fresh mint

1 small mild red onion, thinly sliced crosswise

¼ cup red wine vinegar

6 cups lightly packed mixed bite-size pieces of butter lettuce and radicchio (or all butter lettuce), rinsed and crisped

6 cups lightly packed watercress sprigs, rinsed and crisped

2 medium-size oranges, peeled and thinly sliced crosswise

¼ cup small pitted ripe or Niçoise olives

¼ cup lime juice

About ¼ cup mixed fresh basil and fresh mint leaves (optional)

Salt and pepper

1 In a small pan, combine water, arrowroot, honey, and chopped mint. Bring to a boil over high heat, stirring constantly. Remove from heat and let stand until cold (about 1 hour).

2 Meanwhile, in a large salad bowl, combine onion and vinegar. Let stand for at least 15 minutes or up to 3 hours. Drain, discarding vinegar; separate onion slices into rings.

3 In same salad bowl, combine onion rings, lettuce, radicchio, and watercress; mix lightly. Top with orange slices and olives.

4 Stir lime juice into honey-mint mixture, then pour through a fine wire strainer over salad; discard residue. Garnish with basil and mint leaves, if desired; season to taste with salt and pepper.

makes 8 to 10 servings

per serving: 49 calories, 2 g protein, 11 g carbohydrates, 0.6 g total fat, 0 mg cholesterol, 49 mg sodium

curry oil

preparation time: About 10 minutes

¼ cup curry powder

1 cup vegetable oil or olive oil

1 to 3 cinnamon sticks (*each* about 3 inches long)

1 In a small pan, whisk together curry powder and ¼ cup of the oil until well blended. Gradually whisk in remaining ¾ cup oil. Add cinnamon stick(s). Heat over medium heat, stirring often, just until warm (not hot or boiling). Remove from heat and let cool slightly.

2 With a clean, dry slotted spoon, lift out cinnamon stick(s); set aside. Carefully pour oil into a clean, dry glass bottle or jar, leaving curry sediment behind; discard sediment. (Or strain oil, if desired.) Add cinnamon stick(s) to bottle; cover airtight and store for up to 6 months.

makes about 1 cup

per tablespoon: 125 calories, 0.2 g protein, 1 g carbohydrates, 14 g total fat, 0 mg cholesterol, 0.8 mg sodium

thai coleslaw

preparation time: about 40 minutes

1/3 cup *each* unseasoned rice vinegar and lime juice

1/4 cup slivered red pickled ginger

2 small fresh serrano or jalapeño chiles, seeded and finely chopped

1 tablespoon *each* sugar and Asian sesame oil

1 tablespoon fish sauce (*nam pla* or *nuoc mam*)

1/2 teaspoon wasabi (green horseradish) powder

2 teaspoons sesame seeds

About 1 pound bok choy (coarse outer leaves removed), rinsed and crisped

1 small red onion, cut into thin slivers

2 medium-size carrots, thinly sliced

8 cups finely slivered Savoy or green cabbage

1 small head radicchio, cut into thin slivers

1 In a small bowl, stir together vinegar, lime juice, ginger, chiles, sugar, oil, fish sauce, and wasabi powder; set aside.

2 Toast sesame seeds in small frying pan over medium-high heat until golden (2 to 4 minutes), stirring often. Pour out of pan and set aside.

3 Thinly slice bok choy and place in a large bowl. Add onion, carrots, cabbage, radicchio, and dressing; mix gently. Sprinkle with sesame seeds.

makes 8 to 12 servings

per serving: 62 calories, 3 g protein, 10 g carbohydrates, 2 g total fat, 0 mg cholesterol, 64 mg sodium

viennese potato salad

preparation time: about 1 hour

2 1/2 pounds small red thin-skinned potatoes, scrubbed

1/2 cup pecan or walnut pieces

3 large red-skinned apples

1/2 cup sliced green onions cup raisins

1/3 cup late-harvest gewürztraminer or Johannesburg Riesling

1/3 cup cider vinegar

2 tablespoons salad oil

1 tablespoon grated lemon peel

2 teaspoons poppy seeds

1 Place unpeeled potatoes in a 5- to 6-quart pan and add enough water to cover. Bring to a boil over high heat; then reduce heat, partially cover, and boil gently until potatoes are tender when pierced (about 25 minutes). Drain, immerse in cold water until cool, and drain again. Cut into 1-inch cubes and set aside.

2 Toast pecans in a wide frying pan over medium-high heat until lightly browned and fragrant (about 3 minutes), stirring often. Pour out of pan and let cool; chop coarsely and set aside.

3 Core 2 of the apples and cut fruit into 1-inch chunks (set remaining apple aside to use for garnish). In a large bowl, combine apple chunks, potatoes, pecans, onions, raisins, wine, vinegar, oil, lemon peel, and poppy seeds; mix gently. If made ahead, cover and refrigerate for up to 6 hours.

4 To serve, mound salad on a large rimmed platter. Core remaining apple and cut into slices; fan slices out next to salad along one side of platter.

makes 6 to 8 servings

per serving: 307 calories, 4 g protein, 51 g carbohydrates, 10 g total fat, 0 mg cholesterol, 15 mg sodium

split pea & green pea salad

preparation time: about 45 minutes

1 cup green split peas

2 cups vegetable broth

½ teaspoon dried thyme

1 package (about 10 oz.) frozen tiny peas (do not thaw)

4 ounces (about 10 tablespoons) dried orzo or other rice-shaped pasta

¼ cup thinly sliced green onions

¼ cup chopped fresh mint

¼ cup vegetable oil

1 teaspoon finely shredded lemon peel

2 tablespoons lemon juice

About 24 large butter lettuce leaves, rinsed and crisped

Mint sprigs

Thyme sprigs

Salt and pepper

1 Sort through split peas, discarding any debris; then rinse and drain peas. In a 1 ½- to 2-quart pan, bring broth to a boil over high heat. Add split peas and dried thyme. Reduce heat, cover, and simmer until split peas are tender to bite (about 25 minutes); drain and discard any remaining cooking liquid. Transfer split peas to a large bowl, add frozen peas, and mix gently but thoroughly. Let stand, stirring occasionally, until mixture is cool (about 3 minutes).

2 Meanwhile, in a 4- to 5-quart pan, bring about 8 cups water to a boil over medium-high heat; stir in pasta and cook until just tender to bite, about 5 minutes. (Or cook pasta according to package directions.) Drain, rinse with cold water, and drain well again. Transfer pasta to bowl with peas. Add onions and chopped mint; mix gently. In a small bowl, beat oil, lemon peel, and lemon juice until blended. Add to pea mixture; mix gently but thoroughly.

3 To serve, line 4 individual plates with lettuce leaves; top each plate equally with pea mixture. Garnish salads with mint and thyme sprigs. Season to taste with salt and pepper.

makes 4 servings

per serving: 458 calories, 19 g protein, 62 g carbohydrates, 15 g total fat, 0 mg cholesterol, 607 mg sodium

cilantro slaw

preparation time: about 15 minutes

8 ounces green cabbage, very finely shredded (about 3 cups)

8 ounces red cabbage, very finely shredded (about 3 cups)

1 cup firmly packed cilantro leaves, minced

¼ cup lime juice

1 tablespoon *each* water and honey

½ teaspoon cumin seeds

Salt and pepper

In a large nonmetal bowl, mix green cabbage, red cabbage, cilantro, lime juice, water, honey, and cumin seeds. Season to taste with salt and pepper. If made ahead, cover and refrigerate for up to 4 hours.

makes 6 servings

per serving: 33 calories, 1 g protein, 8 g carbohydrates, 0.2 g total fat, 0 mg cholesterol, 14 mg sodium

bulgur tabbouleh salad

preparation time: 15 minutes, plus about 1 hour for bulgur to stand

chilling time: at least 30 minutes

2 cups bulgur

1 1/2 cups firmly packed fresh mint leaves

1 can (about 15 oz.) garbanzo beans, drained and rinsed

About 1/2 cup lemon juice (or to taste)

2 tablespoons olive oil

Salt and pepper

About 8 large butter lettuce leaves, rinsed and crisped

2 large firm-ripe tomatoes, thinly sliced

4 ounces feta cheese, crumbled

Mint sprigs and lemon slices

1 In a deep bowl, mix bulgur and 2 cups cold water. Let stand until grain is tender to bite and water has been absorbed (about 1 hour), stirring occasionally.

2 Finely chop mint leaves and add to bulgur along with beans, lemon juice, and oil. Mix well; season to taste with salt and pepper. Cover and refrigerate until cool (at least 30 minutes) or for up to 4 hours.

3 Line a platter with lettuce leaves. Arrange tomatoes around edge of platter; mound tabbouleh in center and sprinkle with cheese. Garnish with mint sprigs and lemon slices.

makes 4 servings

per serving: 486 calories, 18 g protein, 74 g carbohydrates, 16 g total fat, 25 mg cholesterol, 463 mg sodium

peking spinach salad

preparation time: about 35 minutes

12 wonton skins (*each* about 3 inches square)

1/3 cup plum jam

1 tablespoon reduced-sodium soy sauce

3 tablespoons lemon juice

1/2 teaspoon ground cinnamon

6 cups lightly packed stemmed spinach leaves, rinsed and crisped

4 ounces mushrooms, thinly sliced

3/4 cup *each* shredded carrots and lightly packed cilantro sprigs

2 medium-size red-skinned plums, pitted and thinly sliced

1 Cut each wonton skin into quarters. Arrange in a single layer on a greased baking sheet; spray or brush with water. Bake in a 500° oven until golden (about 3 minutes), watching carefully to prevent burning. Set aside.

2 In a small bowl, stir together jam, soy sauce, lemon juice, and cinnamon. Set aside.

3 Place spinach in a large bowl. Top with mushrooms, carrots, cilantro, and plums. Just before serving, add won ton skins and dressing; mix gently and serve immediately.

makes 8 servings

per serving: 99 calories, 3 g protein, 22 g carbohydrates, 0.6 g total fat, 1 mg cholesterol, 196 mg sodium

warm wild rice & asparagus salad

preparation time: 15 minutes
cooking time: about 1 hour and 20 minutes

1 cup wild rice, rinsed and drained

1 cup lentils

1 pound mushrooms, thinly sliced

1 large onion, chopped

About 2 ¹/₂ cups vegetable broth

1 pound slender asparagus

3 tablespoons balsamic vinegar

1 tablespoon olive oil

¹/₂ cup grated Parmesan cheese

1 In a 5- to 6-quart pan, combine rice and 8 cups water. Bring to a boil over high heat; then reduce heat, cover, and simmer for 30 minutes. Meanwhile, sort through lentils, discarding any debris; rinse lentils, drain, and set aside.

2 Add lentils to rice and continue to simmer until both rice and lentils are tender to bite (about 25 more minutes). Drain and let cool.

3 In a wide nonstick frying pan, combine mushrooms, onion, and ³/₄ cup of the broth. Cook over medium-high heat, stirring often, until liquid evaporates and browned bits stick to pan bottom (about 10 minutes). To deglaze pan, add ¹/₃ cup of the broth, stirring to loosen browned bits from pan; continue to cook until browned bits form again. Repeat deglazing step about 3 more times or until vegetables are browned, using ¹/₃ cup more broth each time.

4 Snap off and discard tough ends of asparagus; thinly slice stalks. Add asparagus and ¹/₃ cup more broth to mushroom mixture; cook, stirring often, until asparagus is tender-crisp to bite (about 2 minutes).

5 Spoon rice-lentil mixture into a large bowl. Add asparagus mixture, vinegar, and oil; mix gently but thoroughly. Sprinkle with cheese.

makes 8 servings

per serving: 236 calories, 15 g protein, 27 g carbohydrates, 4 g total fat, 4 mg cholesterol, 413 mg sodium

salad of leaves & fruit

preparation time: about 15 minutes

Citrus Dressing (recipe follows)

1 large orange

1 medium-size head butter lettuce, separated
   into leaves, rinsed, and crisped

1 head radicchio or Belgian endive, separated
   into leaves, rinsed, and crisped

1 cup raspberries or seedless red grapes

1 Prepare Citrus Dressing; set aside. Cut peel and all white membrane from orange. Cut between membranes to release orange segments; set aside.

2 Tear lettuce and radicchio leaves into bite-size pieces. Place leaves in a bowl and toss to mix. Then mound leaves equally on 4 individual plates; top with oranges and raspberries. Spoon Citrus Dressing over salads.

makes 4 servings

CITRUS DRESSING

In a small bowl, stir together ¹/₄ cup orange juice, 2 tablespoons raspberry vinegar or red wine vinegar, and ¹/₂ teaspoon honey. Season to taste with salt.

per serving: 61 calories, 2 g protein, 14 g carbohydrates, 0.5 g total fat, 0 mg cholesterol, 5 mg sodium

chicken salad with kumquats

preparation time: about 35 minutes
standing time: about 20 minutes

1 ½ **pounds chicken breast halves, skinned**

Ginger-Mint Dressing (recipe follows)

³/₄ **cup kumquats, thinly sliced, seeds and ends discarded**

1 **small cucumber, cut in half lengthwise, then thinly sliced crosswise**

16 **Belgian endive spears or 8 large radicchio leaves, rinsed and crisped**

Mint sprigs (optional)

1 In a 5- to 6-quart pan, bring about 3 quarts water to a boil over high heat. Rinse chicken and add to water; return to a boil. Then cover pan tightly, remove from heat, and let stand until meat in thickest part is no longer pink; cut to test (about 20 minutes). If chicken is not done after 20 minutes, return it to water, cover pan; and let stand longer, checking at 2- to 3-minute intervals. Remove chicken from water and let cool; then tear meat into shreds and discard bones. (At this point, you may cover and refrigerate until next day.)

2 Prepare Ginger-Mint Dressing

3 Add kumquats to bowl with dressing; mix gently. Mix in cucumber and chicken. On each of 4 individual plates, place 4 endive spears or 2 radicchio leaves; top equally with chicken mixture. Garnish with mint sprigs, if desired.

makes 4 servings

GINGER-MINT DRESSING

In a large bowl, combine ½ cup lemon juice, ¼ cup finely shredded fresh mint or 2 tablespoons dry mint, 2 tablespoons each water and minced crystallized ginger, 2 ½ teaspoons sugar, and 1 tablespoon fish sauce (*nam pla* or *nuoc mam*) or reduced-sodium soy sauce.

per serving: 211 calories, 28 g protein, 21 g carbohydrates, 2 g total fat, 65 mg cholesterol, 90 mg sodium

golden potato salad

preparation time: about 50 minutes
cooling time: about 30 minutes

3 ½ **pounds small red thin-skinned potatoes, scrubbed**

8 **ounces slender green beans, ends removed**

³/₄ **cup chopped yellow bell pepper**

About ¹/₃ **cup low-sodium chicken broth**

3 **tablespoons red wine vinegar**

1 **tablespoon** *each* **balsamic vinegar and olive oil**

1 **teaspoon** *each* **ground turmeric, crushed anise seeds, and dry tarragon**

Salt and pepper

1 Place unpeeled potatoes in a 5- to 6-quart pan and add enough water to cover. Bring to a boil; reduce heat, partially cover, and boil gently until potatoes are tender when pierced (about 25 minutes). Lift out with a slotted spoon and let stand until cool (about 30 minutes). Meanwhile, return water in pan to a boil over high heat. Add beans and cook, uncovered, just until tender-crisp to bite (2 to 3 minutes). Drain, immerse in cold water until cool, and drain again. Cut potatoes into ½-inch-thick slices; cut beans into 1-inch lengths.

2 In a large bowl, combine bell pepper, ⅓ cup of the broth, red wine vinegar, balsamic vinegar, oil, turmeric, anise seeds, and tarragon. Add potatoes and beans; mix gently. For a moister salad, add a little more broth. Season to taste with salt and pepper.

makes 8 servings

per serving: 190 calories, 5 g protein, 39 g carbohydrates, 2 g total fat, 0 mg cholesterol, 19 mg sodium

index